W9-BIE-608

# A
# SPLENDID
# MADNESS

# ALSO BY THOMAS FRONCEK

As AUTHOR

*Home Again, Home Again: A Son's Memoir,* 1996

*Take Away One,* 1985

*The Northmen,* 1976

As EDITOR

*Sail, Steam and Splendour:*
*A Picture History of Life Aboard*
*the TransAtlantic Liners,* 1977

*The City of Washington:*
*An Illustrated History,* 1976

*Voices from the Wilderness:*
*The Frontierman's Own Story,* 1974

*The Horizon Book of the Arts of Russia,* 1970

*The Horizon Book of the Arts of China,* 1969

# A SPLENDID MADNESS

## A MAN · A BOAT · A LOVE STORY

## THOMAS FRONCEK

SHERIDAN HOUSE

First published 2004
in the United States of America by
Sheridan House, Inc.
145 Palisade Street
Dobbs Ferry, NY 10522
www.sheridanhouse.com

Copyright © 2004 by Thomas Froncek
Photos by the author unless otherwise indicated

Portions of this book have appeared in *SAIL* and *Good Old Boat* magazines

All rights reserved. No part of this publication
may be reproduced, stored in any retrieval system
or transmitted in any form by any means, electronic,
mechanical, photocopying, recording, or otherwise,
without the prior permission in writing of Sheridan House.

*Library of Congress Cataloging-in-Publication Data*

Froncek, Thomas.
    A splendid madness: a man, a boat, a love story /
Thomas Froncek.
        p. cm
Includes bibliographical references.
ISBN 1-57409-179-4 (alk. paper)
    1. Froncek, Thomas. 2. Sailors—United States—Biography.
3. Sailing. I. Title.
GV810.92.F76 A3 2004
797.1'24'092—dc22                                    2003019669

Edited by Janine Simon
Designed by Jesse Sanchez

ISBN 1-57409-179-4

# ACKNOWLEDGEMENTS

No one truly sails solo. No boat was ever steered, no life was ever fully lived and no book was ever brought to completion without the help and support of others: teachers, colleagues, friends, family. In all these I have been a fortunate sailor and I am enormously grateful to the many people who guided me on my way.

My thanks first of all to Diego Carr, a wise, patient and inspiring teacher, who first showed me the ropes. Thanks to Neil Murdock, who so graciously offered his time and good counsel (and help with the motor) when ADVANCE and I were just beginning our life together. Thanks to the gang at the Nyack Boat Club, especially Kieran Quinn, Vin Landers, Al Gordon, George Lechman, Morris Azar, Paul Kisala, Elaine Hinsch, Howard Rinehart, Simon Faucard, Jon and Carol Marsh and Steve and Judy Sellinger. A beginning sailor could not hope for better guides or companions. Thanks also to Walter Teurs and Bob Schneider for keeping ADVANCE on the water even when all hope seemed lost, and to Jeff Levy and Irwin Kwartler for their help with the photo shoot.

I am grateful as well to the crew at Petersen's Boat Yard in Upper Nyack, especially Christina and Dave, and also to George and Barbara at Samelot Marine in Haverstraw. Whenever I called upon them at times of mechanical distress they were invariably cheerful with their advice and generous with their hands-on asistance.

For their professional help in seeing this book through to publication I am deeply indebted to Bill Reiss, a careful and able counselor and a loyal friend, and to Sally Arteseros who gave me invaluable guidance when the manuscript needed scraping, painting and varnishing. Thanks to Marty and Judy Cohen for their close reading and good suggestions, and to John Charters of the Tanzer Association for the vintage Tanzer promotional materials that appear in this book. I am grateful also to Lothar Simon at Sheridan House for his encouragement, enthusiasm and publishing professionalism.

Finally, my love and gratitude to Ellen, Jesse and Linda. They were not always eager sailors, but without their love and encouragement my voyaging would not have been nearly as much fun.

*For Ellen,*
*who shares the voyage*

*Mr. Scott:* We find people fond of being sailors.

*Dr. Johnson:* I cannot account for that, any more than
   I can account for other strange perversions of imagination.

—Boswell's *Life of Johnson*

# CONTENTS

# THE HAPPIEST DAY

*"Keep not standing fixed and rooted.*
*Briskly venture, briskly roam."*
  —*Goethe*

It was like being slapped hard by a big wet hand. One second I was upright, in full control, breezing along nicely, the wind in my hair, a grin on my face. At that moment I had no doubt that I was the happiest man in the world.

For the first time in my life I was out on the water in a boat I could call my own. I was not part of anyone else's crew. I was not a student, cramped in a small cockpit with four or five others, waiting my turn to do something interesting. I was not a renter paying by the hour for the privilege of borrowing a piece of someone else's dream. This boat was mine. I was owner and skipper, able to go where and when I pleased. From bow to stern, from the weighted keel beneath the waves to the topmast scraping the clouds, she belonged to no one but me. Her main and foresail puffed out smartly, like the starched shirtfronts of a pair of portly moguls. And the tiller fit my hand perfectly. Balanced between wind and water, my nimble little craft responded instantly to my touch, turning and gliding as gracefully as a ballroom dancer.

Mine. Like the sunshine on my shoulder, and the wind that was pulling me along, and the spray showering off the bow like fistfuls of diamonds. All mine. After all this time. After all the waiting and yearning and delay, after all the sensible planning and deferring and putting off. Mine. At last. And I was savoring every moment of proud possession, every puff of my wind, every splash of my prow in my waves.

That's when I got smacked.

Had I been the least bit superstitious, I might have imagined that someone had heard me laying claim to things that did not belong to me. Oh, so you think all this is yours, do you? This sunshine? This blessed wind? These joyous, tossing waves? Yours to command? Well, think again, bucko.

I should have seen it coming. That dark patch on the water should have been a warning. I had sailed enough on other people's boats to know what it meant. A gust of wind had its claws on the water and it was headed my way. But I was too caught up in my possessive reverie, too sure of myself. Too happy.

The burst of wind hit so fast and so hard that the boat was knocked over in less time than it takes to tell it. My cap flew off and went spinning away. Water was poring into the cockpit and over my sneakers. The bottom edges of the sails were dragging in the foam and I was pulling on a tiller that suddenly seemed to weigh a thousand pounds. With water sloshing around my ankles and the wind howling in my ears, I was being carried along like a leaf in a gale and all I could do was hang on for dear life and wonder what in holy hell I'd gotten myself into.

When does an interest become an obsession? At what point does mild curiosity slip over the line into indecent fervor? When does infatuation turn to adultery? When does experimentation become addiction?

Ask a philanderer and you might get some answers. Ask a junkie, or a serial killer, or a collector of Hummel figurines. Maybe they could help. But back then, if you had asked me how it happened that I found myself being overtaken by an all-consuming passion for things nautical you'd have gotten zip—a dumb stare and nothing more.

The fact is, no one—not my wife, my son, my friends or

anyone I knew who was not already a boat fiend—was more surprised than I to discover that I had let myself get caught up in something so utterly impractical, so foolishly spend-thrift of time and money. Normally I am a pretty level-headed guy: responsible; easy-going; not easily swept away by passions of the head or the heart. Eventually I was to discover that my malady was perfectly understandable to other boat addicts. But at the beginning I thought I was a nutcase unto myself. My family had no doubt whatever.

What made the whole business so baffling was that I had never been a sporty kind of guy. It wasn't just that I lacked any interest in football, baseball, basketball or other popular sports. Thanks to the multiple humiliations of high school phys ed classes—bullying coaches, hectoring teammates, fumbles, fouls, stumbles and strikeouts—I had a deep-seated aversion to any and all group sporting events. At various times I had attempted tennis and golf, but my enthusiasm had been short-lived. Any enjoyment I might have had was undermined by bad ankles and pathetic scores, and by the fact that I just didn't care enough to get better. Hiking in the hills had been more my style: solitary, no-equipment-necessary, find-your-own-path rambles, with no one measuring how far or how long or how fast I went, and with no one keeping score.

That same urge for independence was surely at work on that day fifteen years ago when, leafing through the local newspaper, my eye fell on an article about a nearby sailing school: "Classes for beginners. . . . Experienced teachers . . . Hundreds have learned to sail."

The photo of the school's owner showed a smiling, round-faced guy standing on a dock before a gleaming forest of masts.

It's odd how things happen, and why. Had it been some other time in my life, or some other place, I doubt I would have lingered on the page long enough to read even the first paragraph. But that day something piqued my interest. I kept reading. It was as if the guy in the photo were speaking directly to me, inviting me to call.

I picked up the phone.

I didn't know it then, but that was the beginning of an obsession that would soon take over my dreams, my imagination, and my spare time. It would also land me in more than a little trouble.

# 1

# GETTING STARTED

*"When the student is ready, the teacher will appear."*
*—Taoist teaching*

He began with the basics: a toy boat made from an oblong block of wood with a point at one end and with a little paper sail glued to a little wooden mast. As I and my fellow students watched, Diego set the toy boat at the center of a cardboard circle. The circle was marked with the points of the compass. A red cardboard arrow showed us the wind direction.

"When the boat is headed directly into the wind, we'll call that position one," Diego said, pointing the bow of the little boat so that it faced the red arrow. "Position two is when the boat is turned away from the wind just enough for the sails to start filling. Like this." He made another adjustment to the direction of the little boat.

*This is pathetic*, I thought. I knew the course was called "Basic Sailing," but this was kindergarten stuff. I was here to sail, not to sit indoors playing with a stupid toy. I wanted to get out on the water. I wanted the real thing.

But I smothered my impatience. I was there to learn, and since this seemed to be part of the process, I'd put up with it. Besides, the weather that day wasn't exactly great for sailing. Outside the window, a cold, wind-driven rain cast a gray haze over the marina. We were on the western shore of the Hudson River, some twenty-five miles north of New York City at a place called Haverstraw Bay. Three-and-a-half miles across and set amid rolling hills, the bay was the widest and certainly one of the prettiest stretches of the Hudson.

Cruising on
Haverstraw Bay
with my new boat
club buddy
Vin Landers in
his Cal 28, CARTE
BLANCHE.
*Photo by
James Mangano*

It was also one of the windiest, and on that day in early
April the wind was so strong that even through the closed
window you could hear it whistling in the rigging of the sailboats that lay in their slips out in the marina.

"It should clear in another hour or so," Diego had told
us when we arrived that morning for our first class. "Until
then, there are some things we can do inside."

In our classroom the weather was only marginally better
than it was outdoors. The tiny, whitewashed room was the
headquarters of the Great Hudson Sailing School. It was little more than a shed, with a low ceiling and fiberboard
walls. In the morning chill, the small electric heater in the
corner threw off barely enough heat to keep our breath from
clouding in front of our faces.

When I signed up for these classes, I had wondered whether the "Great" in the school's title referred to the Hudson or to the school itself. I learned the answer that morning, as soon as I stepped inside the cramped little office, with its second-hand chairs and its battered desk strewn with paperwork, boating magazines, equipment catalogues, old paper cups and overflowing ashtrays. The river was far greater than the sum of these parts.

Still, there was something reassuring about the clutter. Despite the school's prepossessing name, the place has a certain laid-back charm that felt just right for a beginner like me. Intimidating it was not.

But it was cold. As I watched Diego pivoting his little boat around on the compass card, I was glad that I had picked up hot coffee on the way over. It not only kept my eyes open on that dreary Sunday morning, it also kept my hands warm. I realized I should have worn a heavier jacket over my woolen sweater. Even so, I felt overdressed compared to Diego, who either didn't feel the cold or was doing a good job of ignoring it.

Lean and fiftyish, with pronounced cheekbones and slate-gray eyes, Diego was dressed more for mid-summer than for early April: torn cotton sweater over a T-shirt; jeans; battered topsiders without socks. No tightly zipped jacket for this guy; no shivering hands clasped around a steaming cup.

Okay, I'll confess. When I learned that my teacher would be someone named Diego, I envisioned olive skin, black hair, a Pancho Villa moustache, volatile temperament. I was wrong on all counts. Whatever Latin genes Diego carried, you couldn't tell by looking at him. The darkness of his complexion suggested a heritage more of weather than of ancestors, and there seemed to be more of bedrock New England than Iberia in those prominent cheekbones, that fair hair. Ditto for his reserved manner and his laconic last name: Carr. What's his story, I wondered. Latin mother and Yankee

father? And from which of them did he inherit the stony sto-
icism that allowed him to shrug off the chill and damp? With
him, I suspected, any grousing about the day's discomforts
was likely to get you written down as a candy ass. Which is
why I, for one, kept my lip as well as my windbreaker zipped
up tight.

Not Marge, though. The only female student in our little
group, she kept making shivering noises and muttering
things like: "Gawd, I'm freezing my tail off."

"I guess now we know why classes are half price in
April," said her husband, Barry, smiling gamely through
clenched teeth.

"You got it," Diego said.

The corners of Marge's mouth drooped even further.

To look at them you'd have thought Marge and Barry
were the perfect couple. Middle thirties. Middle height. Middle to upper income. Their clothes were crisply new and em-
blazoned with fashionable labels. Their brightly colored
windbreakers showed no stains or wrinkles. Their canvas
deck shoes were brilliantly white and showed not a scuff or
a smudge. Their boat, too, was brand new, as we had
learned earlier when Diego had asked us all why we had
come and what we expected to get out of these lessons. Barry
had gone first.

"We're buying a boat," he said. "A Pearson twenty-five.
She's brand new, right out of the shop."

"Nice," Diego said.

"And I want Marge to be part of it," Barry continued.
"She wants to learn the ropes. Right, honey?" He threw his
wife a patronizing smile. He didn't quite call her "little
woman," but I had a feeling the words were on the tip of his
tongue.

I didn't know a Pearson from an Edsel, but I knew I was
meant to be impressed by Barry's choice. And I was. In a
dark corner of my soul I felt the stirrings of envy and something like resentment. How come a young guy like him could

afford a twenty-five foot yacht? Had he hit it big on Wall Street? Inherited a fortune? Made some sort of software breakthrough?

"What about you, Tom?" Diego asked.

I shrugged. How could I explain the impulse that had brought me here? "Oh, I sailed a little in college and really enjoyed it," I began, groping. "And, well, I thought it might be fun to pick it up again." I shrugged again, helpless in the face of life's unfathomable mysteries.

"Okay," said Diego, as if what I'd said made perfect sense. "Pete? What brings you here?"

The fourth student in our group was a skinny young guy, probably in his late twenties, who I immediately pegged as Blackbeard because of the thick dark fringe that concealed the lower half of his face. A mop of dark hair did the same for Pete's forehead. About all you could see peeking through

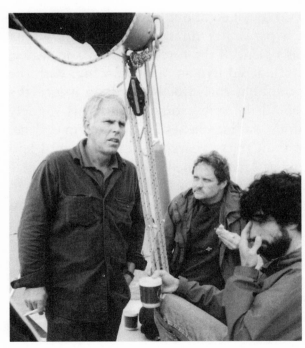

Sailing instructor Diego Carr (standing) shares tips on seamanship with my fellow students during a coastal cruising class on Long Island Sound.

9

the shrubbery was a pair of startlingly blue eyes: robin's eggs in a wooly nest.

Like me, Pete had done a little sailing and wanted to learn more. He dreamed of someday owning a boat, but for now he was happy just to sail. He seemed sensible, unpretentious and a little shy. Once the introductions were over he hardly said a word for the rest of the morning.

"When the wind is coming over the side of the boat, but still from the front—like this—we'll call that position three," Diego continued now, maneuvering his little toy. "Position four is when the wind is coming directly over the side. Position five: wind over the back quarter. And when the wind is from directly behind, that's position six. There are names for all of these positions, okay? You've probably heard some of them: close hauled, beam reach—all that nautical stuff. But for this class we'll keep things simple."

During the next hour or so Diego ran through various lessons and theories. He talked about how to adjust the tiller and sails to go in a particular direction; about the way a boat's keel and sails balanced the forces of wind and water; about the way the sail acted like an airplane wing, with the wind not pushing the boat forward, but pulling it into the vacuum created behind the sails. Some of this was vaguely familiar to me from the sailing classes I had taken in college. But that was more than thirty years ago and by now I had forgotten most of what I had learned.

"I know it sounds complicated in the abstract," Diego continued. "But it'll start making sense once we get out on the water."

At that moment, as if on cue, the sun broke through the overcast, lighting up the marina. Outside our classroom window the rigging sparkled and the white boats gleamed.

"Perfect timing," said Diego. "Let's head out to the dock."

"Just when I was getting warm," muttered Marge. But

she dutifully joined the parade as Diego ushered us out the door and over to a gate that marked the entrance to the marina. He punched a series of numbers into an electronic keypad mounted on a post. The gate swung open and . . . we stepped into another world.

I doubt that Dorothy was any more enchanted with her first view of the Emerald City than I was with my first inside look at a real marina. Until then I had only ever seen such places from a distance: a passing glimpse from the road or from the other side of a chain link fence. But as Diego led the way along a maze of docks and piers—"Careful. These surfaces are still wet from the rain."—I dawdled behind, entranced by the wonderful new sights around me.

I was surrounded by boats, hundreds of them. Some of the motor yachts were as big as houses, with decks so high above the dock that they could only be reached by climbing a flight of steps. I saw gleaming hulls, polished wooden rails, sparkling chrome fittings. Stealing glances through windows fitted with Venetian blinds, I glimpsed lounges larger than my living room. They were furnished with plush easy chairs, TV sets and wet bars. The dinghies that were tied down on some top decks were themselves the size of small yachts.

But it was the sailboats that held my attention. The largest of them had masts that towered sixty feet or more above their decks, with thrusting bowsprits and yards of polished teak handrails. And what complex machines they were, with intimidating arrays of ropes, wires, cables, winches, shackles, cleats and dozens of other gadgets that I could not name. Envy was pointless. Even if I had the money to make one of these beauties my own, I wouldn't have a clue how to handle one. It would take a lifetime of learning to manage boats like these, and I was starting way late.

But there was no need to despair. As I strolled along, other possibilities beckoned. Tucked in amid the grand knock-your-eyes-out cruisers were whole flotillas of smaller, more modest sailboats. Beside their big flashy sisters they seemed like Cinderellas before the ball: humble, unassuming but with their own distinctive charm and grace. They looked as if they might be manageable—with a little practice.

It was time to stop daydreaming and to catch up with Diego and the others.

The marina was laid out in an orderly grid, like a subdivision. A broad main dock served as a kind of boulevard, providing access to a succession of four or five color-coded avenues of permanent docks. Each avenue in turn gave access to several dozen small finger docks: little cul-de-sacs that offered parking spaces where boats could tie up.

I found my classmates at the far end of the blue-colored avenue. They were crowded together on a finger dock, where a spanking new sailboat was tied up. Diego was already aboard.

The boat was not a gaudy giant, but she was no peanut either. She filled the slip from end to end. Painted on her hull were the words Beneteau First 25. This was not her name, as I later learned, but the name of the manufacturer (Beneteau), followed by the model (First being the low-end of the Beneteau line), and the length (twenty-five feet overall).

The boat's hull and decks were snowy white and her lines were Ferrari-sleek. Her foredeck and cabin top swept up and back in one sexy, continuous curve, so that it was impossible to tell where the foredeck ended and the cabin top began. The bow, rather than raking back and down in the fashion of the old clipper ships, sliced straight down to the water with all the crisp efficiency of a meat cleaver.

Lucky we. This polished beauty, this graceful object of desire, was the boat we'd be learning on, and I was now more eager than ever to get out on the river. But again Diego had his own schedule in mind. Before inviting us aboard, he teased us with more instructions, more details. I thought: Either this guy is obsessively methodical or he gets a big kick out of foreplay. One thing was certain: He was doing a great job of raising my level of anticipation.

First he showed us where the life preservers were kept and cautioned us on safety matters.

"Whenever you move around on the boat, make sure you're holding onto something," he said. "Remember the rule: One hand for yourself, one hand for the boat."

When climbing aboard, he warned, we should grasp one of the metal guy wires that held up the mast. "Oh, and by the way," he said, "those wires are part of the standing rigging. All the lines that are permanently fixed, like the forestay, the backstay, and the shrouds—they are the boat's standing rigging."

"Shrouds?" Marge asked.

I wondered, too. The term sounded suspiciously funereal.

"They're the guy wires that brace the mast from the sides. The forestay and backstay"—he pointed to the cables angling down from the top of the mast to the bow and stern of the boat respectively—"support the mast at the front and the back. Again, that's the standing rigging. Running rigging refers to all the lines that move, the ones that you use to run the boat. Okay? That includes the halyards—the lines that raise the sails—and the sheets, which are used to pull the sails in closer to the boat's centerline or to let them out further."

"Should we be taking notes?" Pete asked, frowning.

Diego cracked a grin. "You mean will it be on the test?"

I had been wondering the same thing. Although I'd been following Diego's explanations to this point, I doubted I'd remember all the stuff he was throwing our way.

He waved our concerns aside. "Forget the terminology. There are thousands of words connected with boats—whole dictionaries full. Most of them have been developed over centuries and they all have perfectly good reasons for being. But you don't have to know any of them to start sailing. If you just point and say 'that blue line over there,' that's fine with me. Don't let the lingo get in your way of learning. Now, come on aboard and we'll take a look at the motor. And don't forget to hang onto the whachamacallit."

"The shroud?" Pete offered.

"That's it," said Diego.

Pete looks pleased. Not me. I had just heard Diego utter a word that filled me with dread. The word was motor. As the others climbed aboard I stayed on the dock—partly because there wasn't room in the cockpit for all of us, and partly because I didn't want to hear what was coming next.

"Now," said Diego, "the first thing you want to do before leaving the dock is check the motor and your fuel supply. You want to make sure you can get back if the wind dies."

He proceeded to rattle off the steps needed to get the outboard started: check this, squeeze that, turn the handle this way, push this button.

I made an effort to pay attention. I knew I'd need to learn this stuff. But motors and I have never been on friendly terms. If there is such a thing as a motor-friendly gene, my father must have left it on the bedside table the night I was conceived. When it came to motors, he was a genius, a master of the moving part, a wizard of the toolbox. In his hands a wrench or screwdriver was a magician's wand. He changed spark plugs and electrical cables as easily as I changed my socks.

To my mind, though, motors were mysterious and dangerous things. I avoided them as assiduously as I avoided sports. In high school, a ten-year-old Pontiac was my chariot of freedom, my American dream machine, and I spent hours keeping her clean and shiny. I even learned how to change the oil and give her a jump start. But whatever else went on under the hood I didn't want to know.

Probably I was reluctant to learn more about motors for the simple reason that my father was such a whiz with them. Given the many conflicts between us, I was in no hurry to follow in his footsteps. Not for me the dirty fingernails, the greasy trousers. I had taken a different direction, making a career for myself as an editor and writer. Instead of spending my days on my back beneath a car, I sat at a desk. About the only grease I ever saw was the butter that dripped onto my manuscripts from my morning bagel.

Now here was Diego, leading us through the workings of an outboard. Yeah, okay, I could see that you needed a motor to get in and out of the marina. And I knew that at some point I'd have to learn how to handle the damn things. But why now? Today all I wanted to know was wind and water, ropes and sails.

As Diego droned on, I let my attention wander over to the open water beyond the marina, where the rain squall had passed and the waves were sparkling in the morning sun. Only when I heard the motor kick in did I drag my attention back to the task at hand.

With the outboard idling and spewing fumes, Diego led us through the next step in the process: leaving the dock. Again, there was a flurry of procedures to keep in mind: the correct sequence for letting loose the dock lines (determined by the wind and current); the right way to turn the tiller, which was just the opposite of what you'd expect.

"I know it all sounds confusing," Diego said, "but you'll get a feel for it. So, who's going to steer us out of here? Marge? Wanna give it a shot?"

To my surprise she did not decline. In fact, she seemed almost eager to take up the challenge.

Following Diego's instructions, I cast off the dock lines, gave the boat a backwards shove, then climbed aboard.

With no room in the crowded cockpit, I took up a position on the cabin steps, standing with my elbows resting on the cabin top. It was from there that I watched Marge put the motor in reverse, goose the throttle, and ease us backwards out of the slip. Straight back. Toward the stern of a big yacht that was parked on the opposite side of the channel.

"Jesus, Marge, watch it!" Barry exclaimed.

"Oops," she said, and quickly turns the tiller, but in the wrong direction.

"The other way," Diego said quietly.

"Shit," Marge said. Overcorrecting, she swung us around and brought our bow to within a few feet of the boat in the adjoining slip.

"Ohh," she said, looking frantic as she backed us out into the channel again.

"What the hell are you doing?" barked Barry.

"Shut up," she snapped.

Great, I thought. That's all we need: a catfight. And we haven't even left the marina yet. Is this fun or what?

Marge was again steering us backwards, this time towards the stern of yet another parked boat. There was a man on board, bent over, tending to something in his cockpit. Hearing the voices, he came erect. He had a wrench in one hand and was paying very close attention as Marge continued backing toward his hull. On other boats, too, people had stopped to watch, no doubt wondering which of them would be Marge's next target.

But as the gap closed between us and the other boat, Diego quietly guided us out of danger. "Take it easy," he said soothingly. "Throttle down, put her in forward gear. Good. Now slowly throttle up again. Slowly, slowly. Good. And don't forget to steer. Straighten her out. That's it."

At last we were going forward up the middle of the channel.

From where I stood on the cabin step I saw that another boater was just beginning to back out of his slip. If he kept coming he'd be right in our path. I glanced back at Diego to see if he'd noticed. He had, but he didn't look worried. Only the fact that he was lighting up a cigarette suggested that his nerves might finally be getting to him.

"It's okay," he told Marge. "He sees you. You can keep going."

How Diego remained so calm I couldn't imagine. If this had been my boat, I'd have been a nervous wreck. But Diego's light touch was paying off. Without any further guidance, Marge steered us gingerly down the center of the channel. Her brow was furrowed in concentration, but she succeeded in avoiding the docks and boats on either side.

Clearing the dock area at last, Margo steered us into the main channel. A few moments later we passed through the mouth of the marina and emerged into open water.

If the sails had been up, I'm sure our collective sigh of relief would have filled them nicely.

Grudgingly I admitted that Marge deserved credit. She'd had the guts to step forward and do the job, and she had done it well.

We were in open water at last, with the motor growling and the breeze in our faces smelling river sweet and with the whole wide expanse of Haverstraw Bay spread before us. To the north, around the next point of land, I could see the narrow gap, like the neck in a bottle, that I knew led upriver to the steep hills of the Hudson Highlands and on to the Catskills, Albany and, finally, to the river's birthplace in the High Peaks of the Adirondack Mountains. To the east, four miles and more across the bay, lay the low, rolling hills of Westchester County, echoing the hills behind us on the western shore. To the south, to our right, spread the rest of the great bay, leading downstream through the broad reaches of the inland sea the Dutch called the Tappan Zee and on south along the cliffs of the Palisades to New York Harbor and the Atlantic Ocean beyond. To my landlocked eyes it was a thrilling panorama. A whole world of water lay open before us. Between here and the broad ocean there were no obstacles in sight—well, almost none. I looked again and saw a red buoy lying directly in our path.

"Watch your heading," Diego quietly warned. "Stay this side of the channel marker."

"Right," Marge said, her brow furrowed in concentration. Pushing the tiller to one side, she turned our bow away so that we missed the buoy by a safe margin.

A few minutes later we slipped out into the open river, beyond the shelter of the point that guarded the harbor. A northwest breeze was kicking up a light chop and as soon as we cleared the point the breeze hit us, throwing waves against the side of the boat.

"Okay, now head up into the wind," Diego says. "Tom, Pete, stand by the sails."

"Aye, aye, sir," said I.

As Marge turned us into the breeze, then slowed the motor, I climbed up to the cabin top and forward to the mast, where various ropes were looped over various hooks. Diego pointed me to the right line and told me to be ready to pull. Pete got busy undoing the ties that secured the mainsail to the boom.

Then it was my turn. Unhitching the main halyard from its cleat on the side of the mast, I gave it a tug, then another and another. As I happily watched the sail rise up the mast, I suddenly recalled doing this same thing before, in what seemed like another life. Decades earlier, in college, I had taken a semester of sailing classes, and the sweet memory of those days came flooding back to me now. At the same time, the rhythm of my movements brought to mind the words of a centuries-old sea shanty that my wife Ellen and I were fond of singing on car trips to coastal New England:

> Way, haul away, we'll haul for better weather.
> Way, haul away, we'll haul away, Joe.

Until now, I had only ever heard the song as a charming artifact. But today I felt in every muscle the shanty's connection to its working origins. It was as if its rhythms had been stored in my brain and body all along, a vestige of a vanished world. I wonder: Will anyone a hundred years from now be singing classic work songs from the office? What is the rhythm of pushing a pen or typing an e-mail? Will any song ever memorialize the corporate brain-storming session? I'm afraid that in our rush to technology we have lost something precious.

At last the sail was up as far as it would go, flapping in the breeze like a bed sheet on a clothesline. Diego showed me how to secure the halyard: wrap it around the mast cleat in a figure-eight, then give the free end an underhand loop, hook it over the cleat and yank it tight.

Next, Pete hauled on the line that unfurled the big foresail. He wrapped the line around a winch on the bulkhead and cleated it off. At Diego's order, Margo cut the motor and we were left in the blessed silence, with only the sound of the wind in our ears. Then Barry, taking the tiller, turned the bow away from the wind. The reaction was immediate. The wind took hold of the sails and the boat leaned over.

We were off! Under sail at last! I had the wind in my face, the sweet river air filling my nostrils, our bow cleaving the waves, our sails brushing the sky. This, *this* was what I'd come for: To be here, in this place and in this moment, wrapped in the sights and sounds and smells of the river, and not wishing that I was somewhere else because for once I was exactly where I wanted to be.

# 2

# THE BUG

*"If a man must be obsessed by something, I suppose
a boat is as good as anything, perhaps a bit better than
most."*
                                        —E.B. White

I was not born to boats. Mine was not one of those families
cursed or lucky enough to have made its living from the sea.
Among my forebears there are no Gloucester fishermen, no
spit-and-polish Annapolis grads, no Louisiana shrimpers, no
fair-haired yachtsmen with bloodlines going back to the
Mayflower. My grandfathers encountered blue water just
long enough to escape the poverty and repression of Eastern
Europe. They crossed the Atlantic as passengers in steerage,
and once safely across they headed inland, settling about as
far from salt water as the continent allows.

So how did it happen? Where did this obsession of mine
come from? How did a guy from the landlocked Middle
West end up fighting to stay aboard a sailboat in a sudden
East Coast blow, teeth gritted and knuckles white?

Mystified, I groped among the branches of the family
tree, hoping to flush out an ancestor who might have shared
my nautical fixation. I turned up two possibilities. One of
them—my mother's brother, Frank—saw the sea from the
deck of a minesweeper in the Pacific during World War II. As
soon as the war was over, though, Frank stowed his uniform
in a trunk and never set foot on a boat again. He was a good
man, but as an inspiration for the nautical life, Frank came
up short.

That left my godfather, Uncle Ed, who never came up

short in anything. Standing six feet six and weighing something like 300 pounds, Ed was both the eldest and largest of my father's brothers. So big was he that the navy seems to have had trouble finding him a uniform that fit. In the snapshots taken at my christening in August 1942, Ed's bellbottoms barely reach his ankles, while the little sailor hat on his head looks as if it had been swiped from a twelve-year-old. No, Ed was not exactly a model of seagoing glamour. Apparently he never even went near the water. A pharmacist by training, Ed spent the entire war behind the drug counter of a base infirmary. And yet, who knows? On that sunny christening day, as he posed for the camera holding my very small self close to his very large chest, some waterborne magic may have rubbed off his ill-fitting middy blouse and into my scarcely formed consciousness.

Something nautical must have been at work because just a few years later my father was snapping photos of *me* in a sailor suit. There I am around age five, standing on the foredeck of a battle-scarred submarine that was tied up at a dock in Milwaukee. A heroic survivor of the war that had just ended, the sub was on display for visitors, who on that day included my parents, my sister and me. In the photo I am a miniature version of Uncle Ed, right down to the bellbottoms and right up to the little round hat. From the grin on my face it is plain that I was already in thrall to the romance of the sea. The damage had been done. I was infected.

There was still time. If my parents had been more attentive they might have inoculated me against further exposure. But Dad made matters worse. On summer Sundays he'd treat us to picnic trips to the shores of Lake Michigan.

I doubt there are few experiences more destructive to a child's good sense than to be plunked down on a sandy beach and subjected to the sight of an endless expanse of blue water. Given enough time to stand gazing toward the broad horizon, where the water and his own imagination seem to touch the very edge of the sky, that innocent, unsuspecting kid is likely to be transformed into a muddle-headed daydreamer. For inevitably that child's eyes will be drawn to where the white sails dance and turn. And watching them, he will want to be out there with them. The beauty of them, the way they slide along on invisible currents of air, will seem to him as mysterious and miraculous as whatever it is that keeps birds and airplanes on the wing. And he will believe with all the fervor of a priest in prayer that like birds and airplanes those boats can go on forever, sailing over the horizon to all the wonderful places that lay beyond.

Was it those trips to the lakeshore that inspired me, at around age ten, to build my own boat? I knew from picture books and movies how she should look: white and sleek, with graceful lines and billowing sails. In my mind's eye I could already see myself launching her from the banks of the little pond I had found on the edge of a nearby field. First, though, I had to build her.

Gathering scraps of lumber that were left over from one of my father's projects, I borrowed one of his saws and cut the boards into what seemed like the right lengths: about four feet long for the sides and two feet long for the front and back. Then I nailed the boards together.

I was almost finished with the hull when my sister wandered over to see what I was up to.

"Who died?" Joyce asked.

"Huh?" I replied.

"How come you're building a coffin?"

It was maddening. My sister, being fourteen months older than I, thought she was right about everything. I hated that. But now, as I looked again at my creation, I had no choice but to agree with her. The oblong box I had built looked more suitable for burying our dog than for sailing. There was nothing graceful about it. The sides did not curve but stood straight up and down and all the corners met at sharp right angles. And since I did not know how to bend the wood to make a nice pointed bow, the front end looked as flat and boxy as the back end.

Well, too bad. I had done a lot of work and I wasn't going to quit just because of something my dumb sister said. Anyway, once the boat had a mast maybe it would look more like a boat.

Digging around in my father's pile of scrap lumber, I found a post, stood it up at the front of the box, nailed it into place, and braced it on the sides with pieces of old clothesline. An old broom handle, fastened to the mast with bent nails, served as a yardarm. An old bed sheet became my sail, and when I tied it to the yardarm, I felt my heart lift at the sight of the wind catching it and making it billow. I could just imagine it pulling my boat over the surface of the pond.

That never happened, though. I could daydream about my boat gliding over the water, but even I could tell she was not exactly seaworthy. Inside, where the floorboards should have fit snug against the sides, I could see grass poking through. Try to launch her in the pond and she would instantly fill up with water. She might still float, but I knew she would sink the minute I tried to climb aboard. And since I did not yet know how to swim, I would certainly go with her to the bottom, drowned by my own foolishness.

In the end I had to settle for sitting in my boat out on the lawn, putting on a brave face while singing "Yo-ho-ho and a bottle of rum" and trying to persuade my sister to come over and walk the plank.

My dry-land love affair with boats continued into high school, when I discovered the obsessive delights of building models of Great Ships of America's Past. Bent over a newspaper-covered desk, I labored with tweezers and glue to assemble plastic replicas of the MAYFLOWER, the CONSTITUTION, and famous fighting ships of World War II.

My favorite model, though, was COLUMBIA, the yacht that won the America's Cup in 1901. With her raked mast, her enormous sails and her sleek hull, she seemed to be racing even when she was standing still on my desk, and I loved the aura of power and prestige that seemed to be hers.

Not that I had any illusions about the kind of people who owned such wonderful toys. Movie stars, celebrities, heirs to great fortunes—that's who owned sailboats. I could dream and yearn, but I was also realistic enough to understand how unlikely it was that sailing could ever be part of the life of someone like me: me, the sensible son of an erratically employed tool-and-die man who had survived the Depression by the skin of his teeth. Why, I'd never even been on a sailboat. What was I thinking?

Not until I got to college did I begin to see other possibilities. By a stroke of luck I found myself attending a university that just happened to be situated on the shores of a beautiful, large lake, and when I arrived for freshman orientation I was delighted to find a fleet of sailboats tied up at a dock behind the student union.

Was it possible? Sailing came with college? I checked the syllabus. Sure enough, listed among the phys ed options was Sailing 101. I signed up.

Our instructor was a senior named Rick. Or maybe Brick. Or Mick. Anyway, it was one of those hard-edged monikers you'd expect to be worn by someone with his looks, as if from the day of his birth his parents had foreseen the marble jaw, the granite cheekbones and Mt. Rushmore forehead.

Despite his high-steroid name and build, however, Rick—as I'll call him—was blessedly free of the kind of balls-on-the-line attitude I had come to loathe in hired sportsmen. Rather than making sailing an I-win-you-lose feat of prowess, the guy made it fun: a skill to be learned rather than a test of wills. Thanks to Rick's low-key approach, I was able to hear him and learn from him. Best of all, for the first time in my life I found myself actually enjoying a sport.

The boats we practiced on were not much bigger than bathtubs. With their plywood hulls and dark green paint, they looked as if they'd been banged together out of old ping-pong tables. But they were perfect for beginners: easy to handle and so responsive that the least puff of wind would send them skittering off across the lake.

The setup was blessedly simple. You had only a tiller and two sails to worry about: the main and the jib. That was it. Oh, except that before you started, you had to remember to lower the centerboard, otherwise the first gust of wind would knock the boat right over on its side and dump you overboard.

"See, the centerboard helps to counterbalance the sail," Rick explained to the nine or ten of us who were in his class. "It also helps keep the boat from being pushed sideways."

Oh. Okay.

It was something I had never thought about before: how a boat's progress and stability were based on invisible forces acting upon each other.

"What's this rope for?" I asked, grabbing a length of cord that was wrapped around a hook near the base of the mast.

"That's not a rope," Rick said.

I looked at him. Was he being funny? I knew a rope when I saw one. "All right," I said, taking the bait, "so what is it?"

"There aren't any ropes on a boat. All of those," he indicated the array of cords that lay scattered about the boat, some lying loose, some coiled neatly, others wound around various hooks and fitting, "are lines. And every line has its own name, which tells you its function. The one in your hand is a halyard. It's used to hoist the main sail."

Similarly the jib halyard was used to raise the jib, as the small foresail was called.

Other lines, called sheets, were used to adjust the sails horizontally. You eased the sheets or hauled them in, depending on how strong the wind was and which direction it was coming from. There was a main sheet for adjusting the mainsail, and two jib sheets, one on each side of the boat. These ran forward through pulleys to where they connected with the back corner of the jib. The jib flapped free until you pulled on one sheet or the other. When you were sailing with the wind on one side of the boat, the main sail and jib would be puffed out on the downwind side. If you tacked—turned the boat so that the wind was coming over the other side of the bow—the mainsail and the jib naturally would be blown to the opposite side of the boat. Making a turn then became a matter of both steering with the tiller and at the same time adjusting the sheets so that the tension was now on the new downwind side.

"See? Simple," said Rick. But he must have read the doubt on our faces, because he hastened to offer reassurance. "It will all become clear once we get under way," he said.

And he was right. It did become clear. But it didn't become any simpler, not right away. For starters, you had to somehow manage to switch the sails from side to side at the same time you were trying to steer. This was easy enough if you had someone else sailing with you. They could handle the jib sheets while you kept your hand on the tiller. But alone, you had to scramble. Plus, you had to be on the lookout for the boom. When the mainsail came swinging around to the new downwind side of the boat, the boom came with it, and if you weren't paying attention you could get smacked in the head or even knocked overboard. "Boom" was right!

When it came to sailing, "simple" was a relative term.

In those first days, Rick addressed such critical questions as how to trim the sails—sheet them in tighter or loosen them up—so that they'd work to maximum effect. Did the wind come on too strong, filling the sails too much and pushing the boat over so far that you risked capsizing? You could spill some of the wind out of the main by loosening the sheet and letting the sail swing away to leeward. Or you could turn the bow into the wind. In either case, the effect would be the same: you'd be lessening the amount of sail area that was exposed to the wind. With less wind pushing against the sail, the boat would come upright and slow down.

Were you about to collide with another boat? Were you coming into the dock too fast? You could put on the brakes by quickly dumping all the wind out of the sails. All you had to do was let the sheets out all the way or turn the bow into the wind. With nothing to grab onto, the wind would lose its hold on the sails, which would start flapping uselessly. "Luffing," it was called. Suddenly you'd be out of power, with only the boat's momentum to carry you along. If you timed it right, you could then coast easily into the dock.

Did you want to get moving again? You pulled in the sheets and tightened up the sails until the wind caught hold and you had power once more. The trick then was to coordinate your steering with your increase in power, so that when you were getting under way again you didn't hit the dock or another boat.

It was scary, and I certainly did my share of dock bashing. But eventually I started to get a feel of those little boats. I learned to judge their speed and momentum and just how much to let out of sails or sheet them in. I began to pick up the sense of timing that made the difference between a smooth docking and the kind of clumsy performance that so entertained the people watching from shore.

Thanks to Rick I learned that getting where I wanted to go was a matter of keeping the boat's direction and the wind's direction in balance. I learned to watch the surface of the water to see what the wind would be doing next. Ruffles moving toward you across calm water meant a breeze was on its way, its paws just skimming the surface. If the water was already stirred up and you saw a darker patch moving your way, you'd better get ready to get socked by a gust.

Little by little I began to get a feel of how to make the boat go where I wanted it to; how to speed it up or slow it down; how to make the most of the wind, and how to take precautions when the wind came on too strong.

I loved it all. Sailing on that lake turned out to be the perfect antidote to the pressures and frustrations of my budding adulthood: keeping up with class work and deadlines; holding down two jobs to pay my way through; coping with the confusing rituals of dating and mating.

For all its technical complications, sailing offered an escape into simplicity. Where the rest of life was messy and vague and full of compromises, sailing was orderly and knowable. I needed only to raise the sails, slip the dock lines and take the tiller and sheets in hand. Then all the tangled conundrums of life ashore went right out of my head. I could set my own course, take my boat where and when I wanted. All I knew then was wind and water, clouds and sun and the birds overhead, and I wished it could go on forever.

It didn't, of course. When my phys ed requirement was fulfilled, I left sailing behind. This was college. Other sirens beckoned, other opportunities turned up. Politics, theatre, journalism—I tried first one direction, then another, hoping to discover what I wanted to do with my life.

Before long, I was caught up in career, marriage, family. I made my way to the East Coast, acquired a mortgage, car payments, home repairs, school bills. Decades went by without my even thinking about boats. I might admire them as they glided by at one or another of the seaside towns where Ellen and I vacationed: Maine, Cape Cod, the Jersey shore. But in all those years I was no more than a distant spectator. I still thought of boats as playthings for the rich, part of someone else's life, not mine. It wasn't so much that I deferred my dream; it just never really took shape.

Maybe it never would have if we hadn't ended up living by the water: in Nyack, a small Hudson River town twenty-five miles north of New York City. From April through October, hardly a weekend went by when I couldn't look out from our village streets to see sails on the river. And watching them, I'd sometimes wonder what it would be like to be out there in a boat of my own.

It was a ridiculous idea. Even if I could afford a boat, where would I keep it? And did I really want one more thing to take care of, when I had all I could do to keep up with my other obligations.

No, it didn't make sense. Better to put the idea out of my mind. Quit tormenting myself with daydreams.

Which I successfully managed to do—until that day when I picked up the local newspaper and there was that article about the sailing school, with that photo of the owner and the schedule of classes: Four weekend mornings a month, April, May or June. And April was half price.

I thought: Hey, maybe this is what I've been looking for. Why not give it a shot? It might just be a good way to start: no big commitment, just a chance to see if I'd like it.

The timing was good. Ellen was out of the house on Sunday mornings, teaching Sunday school, so I'd go on Sundays. We'd have no conflict about schedules. Perfect.

I reached for the phone, then caught myself. My God, what was I thinking? I'd almost forgotten about that other important part in my life: my writing. Was I about to sabotage myself? Sunday mornings I was almost always at my desk, wrestling with the book that had been filling my head and my spare time for the last several years.

It was a story close to my heart: a memoir about the house my father had built when I was a kid. The place had been nothing fancy: a small ranch-style house set on two acres of prairie on the outskirts of Milwaukee. But it was my father's dream, and in the process of planning and building it, he had given my sister and brother and me a priceless legacy: a sense of possibilities, an unshakable belief that dreams could indeed become realities.

I wanted the book to be a tribute to that legacy and to my father, and getting it done meant keeping to a strict schedule and tedious discipline. On weekday mornings I put in two hours at my desk before going off to my day job at Reader's Digest, where I was an editor in the book department. On Sunday mornings I did no yard work, attended no breakfast socials. I turned down all invitations to join in community softball games or the once-a-week poker games with the guys from the office. When dinner guests stayed too late on Saturday evenings, I excused myself and went to bed. I made no apologies. My writing time came first. Yet here I was, about to give away those precious hours—and for what? Just so I could have a little fun?

I thought of Balzac, who worked eighteen hours a day and became immortal. I thought of Stendhal—or was it Flaubert?—who refused even to have a dog lest caring for it take too much time from his writing. No, this was a job that no one else could do but me. If I didn't keep at it, the book would never get written.

I dithered. I was torn. I wanted to write . . . I wanted to play. I wanted art . . . I wanted life!

The answer came to me in a flash of cold reality. I asked myself: Is it likely that the only thing standing between me and literary acclaim is a little lost work time, a few hundred words on a page?

The answer was clear. The answer was: Nah.

# 3

# A BOW TO THE KING

*"The most beautiful thing we can experience is the mysterious. It is the source of all true art and science."*
—*Albert Einstein*

At first, I didn't know what was happening. It was my turn at the helm on that first Sunday morning class with Diego, and I was trying to steer us south on Haverstraw Bay, following the river toward the sea. A light breeze filled our sails from behind. Water foamed against our bow. A healthy wake trailed our pretty Beneteau. Yet we did not seem to be making any headway. In fact, unless I was mistaken, just the opposite was happening. We were going backwards!

It was embarrassing. As skipper I was supposed to be directing our course. But for the life of me I couldn't make the boat go where I wanted it to go.

To check our progress, I picked out a smoke stack on shore and visually lined it up against the hill that rose behind it. Then I watched to see which way their positions shifted. My hunch was right. Some impish river sprite was toying with us, pushing us back upstream with a gentle but insistent hand. What on earth was going on?

"Watch the buoys," said Diego. "You can tell which way the current is running."

I looked to where he pointed. The nearby channel markers were leaning upriver like drunks on a spree. The water flowing around them cut deep V-shaped ripples on their upstream sides. Or was it their downstream sides? Everything, it seemed, was turned around.

That's when it clicked. We were at the mercy not of some

An early taste of sailing at its best: sunny skies, a fair wind and me at the helm during one of my first sailing lessons on Haverstraw Bay on the lower Hudson River.

playful demon but of a force of nature. "It's the tide, right?" I asked.

"The tidal *current*," Diego corrected.

"There's a difference?"

"A big difference. Tide is the vertical rise and fall of the water. Current is its horizontal movement. In a boat you have to worry about the tide when you're anchoring or going into shallow water or under a bridge. But the current will affect you even when you're out in the middle of the river. You always have to take it into account."

I should have known. I had been to the seashore plenty of times. I had seen how the ocean's rise and fall would leave rocks alternately drowned and uncovered, how it would turn sparkling bays into muddy wastelands. Swimming at the beach, I had felt the pull of the current beneath the surf. But never before had I been in the grip of the Hudson's tidal surge. It seemed utterly foreign to me.

In Wisconsin, where I grew up, rivers did the sensible thing: they all went downhill. Sure, they spent time and energy meandering through the countryside. Sometimes they even turned back on themselves, creating eddies and backwaters. Mainly, though, their current flowed in only one direction. Set yourself adrift in a canoe on a Midwestern river and sooner or later you were bound to end up downstream from where you started.

As for the lakes where Dad sometimes took me fishing in a rowboat—well, lakes didn't do much of anything. Unless the wind stirred things up, you never felt any movement. On a calm day you could sit for hours, fishing pole in hand, without worrying that the current might carry you away.

But the Hudson River was different. In fact, it was not really a river at all. It was an estuary, an arm of the sea that extended some 150 miles inland from New York Harbor to the city of Troy—almost half the river's length.

This is the stretch of river that was first explored in the summer of 1609 by Henry Hudson, the English captain hired by the Dutch East India Company to search out a passage to the "islands of spicery" in the Far East. Encouraged by the width and depth of the water he found at the river's mouth, Hudson sailed his ship, HALF MOON, far inland. And who could blame him for trying? Where it met the sea and for many miles to the north, the route seemed promising indeed: a river broad enough and deep enough to broach a continent. Eventually, though, the channel grew too shallow for HALF MOON to proceed. At about the site of present-day Albany, Hudson realized that wherever the shortcut to the Far East might lie, this was not it. He had no choice but to turn back and try his luck elsewhere.

When Hudson sailed the river, tidewater extended farther upstream than it does today. Fish from the Atlantic swam as far north at Glens Falls, some 210 miles from the sea. Today, the Federal Dam at Troy—first erected in 1826—blocks the northern end of the Hudson estuary. Above the dam, the river is the freshwater child of the Adirondack mountain streams that give it birth. But below the dam it is a tide-driven creature of the sea. True, during the spring runoff, the upper river can still make itself felt. The immense rush of fresh water from the mountains can overwhelm the tide for many miles south of Troy. For most of the year, though, the lower river flow is determined not by gravity but by the twice-daily inhaling and exhaling of the Atlantic tides.

Crisscrossed by currents, active even when it seems to be standing still, the river can seem to be almost a living, breathing creature, pulsing with rhythms set in motion by forces far beyond its shores. And as I was discovering, those powerful submarine realities affect every boater who ventures out onto the lower Hudson, whether he is pushing a paddle, steering a sloop, or piloting a barge from the wheelhouse of a tugboat.

To the natives who were the valley's original inhabitants, the river's twice-daily reversals of direction must have seemed as profoundly mysterious as they did to inlanders like me. The Algonquin tribes called it "The River that Flows Two Ways"—*Muhheahkantuck* in their language—and the reality behind the name still holds true. Try drifting downstream in a canoe on *this* river and you'll soon wish you'd brought a paddle. For every eight miles the current carries you down, the reverse tide will carry you seven and a half miles back up. To coast the 150 miles from Albany to Manhattan without stopping you'd need to pack almost a year's worth of food. Do a Huck Finn on the Hudson? You'd better have plenty of time and patience, and plenty of grub.

Diego made an effort to explain the process. "What happens is, the sun's gravitational force, combined with the moon's gravitational force, pulls up on the earth's surface. The earth is literally pulled out of shape."

To demonstrate, he held his hands as if holding a ball, then pulled them slightly apart. "Mostly we see the effects on the ocean, but the land is being pulled up, too."

Standing at the head of the cockpit, his back to the cabin, Diego could as well have been standing in front of a blackboard. He was in full teaching mode, and as I kept my hand on the tiller and my eyes on the river ahead, I wondered if he had ever been a teacher. He seemed a natural, both in his enthusiasm for his subject and in his gift for encouraging his students without making them feel like idiots.

"Think of the Atlantic as a bowl full of water," he went on. He cupped his hands to show us how it worked. "The sun's gravitational field pulls on its surface at the same time the earth is turning. So the ocean is sort of being dragged across the earth. It's as if that basin of water is being sloshed from side to side. First the water is up on one side of the bowl and down on the other, then it sloshes back to the other side. Same with the tides. When the tide is up on the European side of the Atlantic, it's down on the American side, and vice versa."

For a beginning sailor it was an awesome vision that Diego evoked that morning. Beneath our little boat cosmic forces were at work. Our progress—or lack of it—was being determined by nothing less than the pull of the sun and the moon.

"Cool," said Barry.

I glanced at him. Cool? The word hardly did justice to the tide's grandeur and mystery. To my mind the Psalmist said it far better: "How great are your works, oh Lord, how very subtle your designs."

It was a new world I was entering, with a seemingly endless array of new rules and perceptions. Not only would I need to learn how to manage wind and sails; I also had to be aware of the forces at work *beneath* my boat.

That morning, I had my first inkling of the frustrations that have been experienced by every sailor who ever launched his boat into tidewater. An old ditty says it all:

> The tide ever flowed
> And the wind ever blowed
> From the place that we goed.

So why not turn on the motor? The eight-horse Merc was primed and ready to leap into action at the touch of a button. Why not just go charging down river with all pistons pumping and to hell with the current?

But all of us in the boat that day were determined to resist using the "iron sail." These few hours grabbed from our busy lives were not about getting somewhere fast or overcoming the forces of nature. They were about learning a skill and a boat and a river. They were about finding out how sails worked—or didn't—in varying conditions. They were about learning how to watch and listen and *feel* what the water and the wind were up to, how they were affecting our vessel, and how they might affect it in another hour or two, given what the clouds foretold.

I sensed ancient mysteries here, the lure of secret knowledge. I yearned to penetrate that hidden world, and I was pretty sure I couldn't do that over the growl of a motor.

All right, but what to do about our lack of progress?

There was only one solution.

"Let's head up into the wind a little," Diego said, nodding toward a point of land on the far side of the bay.

Remembering what he had taught us earlier in the day, I pushed the tiller away from me and saw the bow swing toward the point. With my other hand I grabbed the line that controlled the mainsail. What was that damn thing called? The main sheet, that was it! Tugging on the sheet, I yanked the main in closer to the boat's centerline. We were now headed toward the point that Diego had indicated and the wind was blowing in our faces instead of coming over the stern. The only problem was the genoa. The big foresail was flapping wildly, like laundry on a clothesline.

"Barry, you'll want to trim the jenny," Diego said.

Grabbing the jib sheet, Barry gave it a couple of turns around a winch, then tugged at it until the sail was taut.

Immediately I could feel the difference in our ride. The boat leaned over, our speed picked up, and I no longer felt the resistance of the current. It was as if the river sprites were pleased with our new direction and had decided to help us along. True, we weren't headed downstream any longer. But never mind. We'd try again next time.

"Go with the flow." Whoever first offered that pithy bit of advice must have been a tidewater sailor.

Each time we went out with Diego the river taught us a new lesson. One crisp and sunny Sunday morning, when a chilly breeze was giving us a brisk joyride on Haverstraw Bay, we noticed a flock of white sails off in the distance, a mile or more away.

"It looks like a race," Diego said. A steely light sparked in his blue eyes. "Let's see if we can catch 'em."

During a Sunday afternoon cruise on the Hudson, just upstream from the Tappan Zee Bridge, I encountered these small boat racers from the Tarrytown Boat Club.

Catch them? I could not imagine how. They were going away from us and had a huge lead. But off we went, racing upwind in hot pursuit.

A high-speed chase in a sailboat is nothing at all like a car chase in the movies. There are no squealing tires, no roaring engines. What we heard instead was the wind in our ears, the machinegun flap of the back edge of the foresail, and the rush of water along the hull. The boat was heeled, forcing us to brace our feet against the back of the downhill bench. Foaming water licked at the lower rail just inches from our shoes. We were probably going no more than five or six miles per hour. Yet we seemed to be flying. Our aimless joyride had suddenly become positively thrilling. And when I saw that we were closing the gap on the racers, I felt an exhilarating surge of adrenaline. The others felt it too. You could see it in their faces: eyes intent, lips clenched tight.

"Tighten up the main a bit," Diego called. "Trim the genoa. Watch your telltales. Sail your telltales."

"Sail your what?" asked Pete, who was at the tiller just then.

"See those little ribbons flying at the front of the jenny? Red on the left side, green on the right? When they're streaming out horizontally it means the sail is trimmed to its most efficient shape. Then you know you're making the most of the wind."

Diego's coaching gave us a big advantage. So did our size. As we pulled closer we could see that the racing boats were small "day sailers." They had no cabins, just little covered decks up front, and their sails were a lot smaller than ours, which gave them a lot less power. But what really made the difference was Diego's knowledge of the currents. By pointing us on a course that seemed like the long way around, he was keeping us away from the main channel, where the opposing tide was at its strongest.

It wasn't long before we were running neck and neck with the competition. We kept our distance so as not to interfere with the race. But we only fell behind when the little guys turned downwind and hoisted their spinnakers: huge sails that belled out ahead of them like brightly colored parachutes. As they pulled away, with their festive red and green and orange and yellow sails billowing out against the sparkling blue of water and sky, they made such a pretty picture that losing the race almost didn't matter. The spectacle seemed reward enough. Almost.

"We'll get 'em next time," Pete said as we watched the racers go flying away on the wind.

"That was great!" I exclaimed.

"Yeah, cool," said Barry—apparently his highest expression of enthusiasm.

Even Marge's interest seemed to have been turned up a notch. Finally she was grinning instead of frowning.

Diego, once again calm and collected, reached into his pocket for his pack of smokes, then lounged back and lit up, the weary veteran. "Take every chance you get to crew in races," he advised, ever the teacher. "You'll learn more in an hour of racing than in a whole day of just cruising around."

On another Sunday morning, no one else showed up for class but me, so I had Diego and his lessons all to myself. I was a little nervous at first, wanting to do everything right while I was under the full glare of the master's scrutiny. And I did pretty well. I got the motor going without any trouble. I backed us out of the slip without hitting anything. I nosed us through the marina's maze of piers and out into open water. I remembered to turn into the wind before trying to raise the sails. Then it was kill the engine and let the wind do its work, which it did nicely, thank you very much.

"How about if we head upstream this time," I suggested when we were well out in the river.

"Fine with me," Diego replied, lighting up again. "You're the skipper."

I smiled. I liked the sound of that.

We talked then, in a way that we hadn't done when the others were on board. We began with the weather, then the boat, but the conversation soon drifted to more personal topics: our jobs, our families. As I suspected Diego had been a teacher. For twenty-five years he had taught history and social studies to high school kids. But twenty-five years had been enough for him. Whether he had quit or been laid off or taken early retirement was not clear, but he was out of the rat race now and savoring every minute of his freedom. He had no regular nine-to-five job, no family responsibilities. He mentioned a wife, but marriage seemed to be a thing of the past. He mentioned two sons, but they were grown now, with their own families and schedules to keep. Diego, it seemed, had freed himself from all the conventional obligations. Instead, he spent his days around boats: teaching sailing; delivering other people's boats to Florida or the Bahamas for the winter; bringing them back in the spring; coming and going as he pleased.

"These days I only do what I want to do," he declared.

I thought: What a thrilling idea! Here's a guy who is actually living the kind of life most men only dream about. He has thrown off all the hum-drum demands that can wear a guy down—the kind Melville writes of in *Moby Dick* when he describes sea-yearning landsmen who spend "week days pent up in lath and plaster—tied to counters, nailed to benches, clinched to desks." Diego had flown free, and he seemed utterly content: a man at peace with himself, no one's pawn, doing no one's bidding but his own. I was jealous.

And yet I thought I heard an edge on his voice: *"These days I only do what I want to do."* What was it in his tone? Resentment? Petulance, as if daring someone to challenge his proud assertion? Maybe things were not quite as rosy as I wanted to believe. Was Diego a happy man or a burnt-out case?

I did not ask. For one thing it was none of my business. But I also did not want to hear anything that might contradict the appealing fantasy I had constructed in my mind. Boats meant freedom, escape, adventure. And although I knew perfectly well that I was not going to turn my back on the life I had built for some will-o-the-wisp idea of the carefree life, I was also in no hurry to spoil the illusion.

With the help of a nice northwesterly breeze I had steered us to the top of Haverstraw Bay. We were now just off Stony Point, a rocky promontory that juts from the river's western shore. We were out in the open. The point was not blocking our wind. Our sails were full, the breeze was steady, water was foaming against our bow. But as had happened on our first outing, the current once again had us in its grip. We were standing still.

"Whew. Incredible current," I said, proud of my newly acquired knowledge.

A slight smile from Diego. "Yup," he said. He knew all along what I had set us up for, but he wanted me to find out for myself.

The obstacle we faced was one of the tightest on the river and one of the toughest to navigate under sail: a narrow passageway a hundred feet deep and less than half a mile wide. Through this pinch-waisted slot between two rocky points— Stony Point to the west and Verplank Point to the east—the Hudson disgorged the outflow from the scores of rivers and streams that lay to the north. To this torrent was added all the seawater that had been pushed upstream on the last incoming tide. Now, with the tide flowing out again, all that water was pouring through the gap and out into Haverstraw Bay like a faucet gushing into a bathtub. And I had steered us right into the faucet's mouth. Sail upstream? I might as well have tried to sail up the face of Niagara Falls. Only the wind in our sails kept us from being hurtled downstream, mere flotsam on the tide. The breeze held our boat where it was, motionless, like a gull hovering on an updraft, while the flood rushed along beneath us.

That fearsome gap marks the southern gateway to the Hudson Highlands, a spectacular fifteen-mile stretch of wooded mountains and stony crags that is surely one of the most dramatic landscapes in the eastern United States. The views here are so impressive, with such vivid contrasts of light and shadow, heights and depths, that you almost wonder whether what you're seeing is real or whether it is the masterwork of some half-mad set designer who has been blessed with an unlimited budget and a too-florid imagination.

If you knew the Highlands only from the painted evocations of Thomas Cole, Frederick Church and the other nineteenth-century masters of the Hudson River School, you could be forgiven for thinking they had made the whole thing up. Those sunsets! Those romantic vistas! On canvas the effects are positively operatic, what with rocky crags, waterfalls streaming down moonlit hillsides, and ruined castles perched on wooded promontories. Surely no actual landscape could be as spectacular as this. But every bit of it is real: the hills, the waterfalls, even those fantasy castles, private Disney Worlds built by profligate tycoons a hundred years ago.

On the crest of one ridge rises a perfect fairytale castle, all high turrets and steep red roofs. Inspired by the castles on the Rhine, it was concocted by a railroad magnate in 1881, and in its lofty tower Rapunzel would have been right at home.

Turn a corner and you come upon an even more improbable sight: a gleaming white Moorish extravaganza that looks like something right out of the Arabian Nights. Supposedly styled after Spain's Alhambra, Dick's Castle was begun in 1903. The fantasy of a Wall Street financier who later went broke, the place is a sprawling white confection of rounded arches, colored tiles and fountain courtyards.

For something in the Scottish mode you have Bannerman's Castle, a vast red-brick ruin whose high fortress walls are topped by battlements and crenellated towers. Begun in 1908, the place sits on a rocky island at the northern gateway to the Highlands, as if guarding the river against enemy invaders. But it was not enemy gunfire that brought the castle to its present state. The owner, a dealer in military surplus, had the bad judgment to use the castle both as a home and as an arsenal to store powder and ammunition. When an accidental explosion sent a barrage of bullets and shot flying, the castle was reduced overnight to a Gothic ruin. It remains today a picturesque artifact for artists and tourists, and a beacon for boaters.

I knew the Highlands before I knew the river. Ellen and I had often acted as tour guides through the area, driving visiting friends or family along the river roads, stopping at overlooks and historic houses, poking into village shops. I'd hiked along the paths that wound through the forested hills and stood on high ridge tops drinking in the view of summer green or autumn gold hills that rolled on and on to the horizon. Always, no matter how far into the forest I went, I could feel the river nearby. It might be invisible from where I stood, but I knew that all I had to do was walk over that next ridge or around the next bend to catch a glimpse of that blue thread weaving it way through the hilly tapestry.

The river gave depth and color to a landscape that I knew well. But of the river itself I did not know enough even to be intrigued by its mysteries—its rhythms, moods and currents. Those came later, when I began sailing with Diego.

I did know that vivid chapters of America's history had been written in the Highlands. Armies had marched here during the Revolutionary War. Lookouts had kept watch from these hilltops. On a forested hillside above Haverstraw Bay, Benedict Arnold turned traitor, making plans with British Major John Andre to hand over the American fortress at West Point to the British. When the scheme was discovered, Arnold fled down river to British-held New

York. Andre was not so lucky. Captured by the Americans, who found the treasonous plans hidden in his boot, the major was tried, judged a spy, and hanged.

Some of the earliest classics of American literature were inspired by Hudson Valley legends, including Washington Irving's "The Legend of Sleepy Hollow" and "Rip Van Winkle." According to Dutch legend, the thunderstorms on the hill called Dunderberg, just upriver where Diego and I now sailed, were caused by the ghosts of Henry Hudson's crew bowling in the mountains.

Now I wanted to see the Highlands the way Irving and Hudson had seen them: from the deck of a boat. That's why I had steered us to that gushing faucet at Stony Point: to get a look at the valley from water level. But there was no way to get closer. Not today. It was going to have to wait for another time.

"Current is king," Diego said. "There's no escaping it. The best you can do is try to make use of it."

How did they manage it in the old days, I wondered—before power conquered the current? How did anybody ever get anywhere in the face of contrary winds and currents? How did they keep to schedules? How could they plan an arrival or departure? In those days, when the quality of most roads was either poor to lousy, the river was the quickest and most reliable route between New York and the interior. Travelers, farmers and manufacturers depended on boats to transport themselves and their goods. But who could say "I'll be there on Thursday at noon," and expect to be believed?

Later, when I began reading about the river, I discovered just how difficult and unreliable travel on the Hudson could be.

For most of the Hudson's history, travelers and merchants depended mostly on the large sloops that plied the river. Patterned after Dutch canal boats, the typical Hudson River sloop was chunky, broad-beamed, shallow-bottomed.

But what the sloops lacked in grace they made up for in stolid practicality. Sixty-five to seventy-five-feet long, with copious cargo space, they were the tractor trailers of their day. Their broad hulls gave them great stability. With their shallow drafts, they could easily sidle up to small rural docks to pick up cargo and passengers.

But simply adding sails to a canal barge did not necessarily create a seaworthy vessel. At home on the canals of Holland, a barge rode low in the water, between the canal's sheltering banks. Wind was hardly a consideration. But when that same barge is fitted with mast and sails and set upon the broad Hudson on a windy day a skipper would have his hands full trying to keep his boat from capsizing. Shortening sail would help, but in a really stiff wind even a small spread of canvas could make it hard for a shallow-draft boat to remain upright. A deeper keel would have helped, but then the boats would have been limited to deep-water harbors.

The solution appeared in 1815, when a clever Hudson River boat-builder came up with the idea of the retractable centerboard. According to most accounts, the first centerboard boat was a 51-ton sloop built for the Hudson River packet trade. Her name was ADVANCE (perhaps in honor of her high-tech design) and she was built in a boatyard in South Nyack—just a few blocks down the hill from where I now lived.

The centerboard revolutionized river travel. The huge underwater fin effectively counterbalanced the wind's pressure on the sail and helped resist leeway. Yet when the board was winched up into its watertight box within the hull, the big boat could easily navigate in shallow waters.

Even fitted with the new invention, however, the Hudson River sloops still could be flummoxed by the vagaries of the Hudson. According to one account, a sloop named CARO-LINE once made the sixty-mile journey from Manhattan to Fishkill in five hours. At other times, the same trip could take four or five days. Becalmed, there was nothing for a skipper to do but drop anchor and wait for a change in the wind or tide.

A passenger in a hurry would have found it a frustrating time. But then, people seemed to be in less of a hurry in the days before the steamboat appeared. As James Fenimore Cooper reported in 1844,

> . . . the passenger did not hurry on board. . . . He passed his morning saying adieu, and when he repaired to the vessel it was with gentlemanlike leisure. . . . There was no jostling of each other . . . no impertinence manifested, no swearing about missing the eastern or southern boats, or Schenectady, or Saratoga, or Boston trains, on account of a screw being loose. . . . On the contrary, wine and fruit were provided, as if the travellers intended to enjoy themselves; a journey in that day was a fiesta. . . . The vessel usually got aground once at least, and frequently several times a trip; and often a day or two were thus delightfully lost, giving the stranger an opportunity of visiting the surrounding country.

Still, it was certainly better to be becalmed than to encounter some of the other surprises that the Hudson had in store. Several tedious days without a breeze might yield overnight to a blistering gale. The surrounding mountains, which had only yesterday walled off the breeze, would suddenly be turned into ferocious wind tunnels, hurling powerful storms down the valley. Then even the most able of captains and the sturdiest of boats could be overwhelmed. Capsizing, sinking and death were not uncommon. The narrow stretch of river at the upper end of the Highlands was especially dangerous—and still is. Here the north winds ricochet off the slopes of Storm King Mountain on the west and Breakneck Ridge on the east, turning the river below into a cauldron of cross currents and whitecaps. So lethal was this stretch of river that the Dutch called it Martyr's Reach.

Something had to give. River travel was too important to the region's growing economy to be held hostage to the whims of nature.

What gave was a contraption that was described as looking like a "backwoods saw-mill mounted on a scow and set on fire," as one observer described Robert Fulton's CLERMONT, which first appeared on the river in August 1807, its stacks belching flame and fire. One farmer thought he saw "the devil going up the river in a sawmill."

Another observer wrote: "The terrific spectacle, particularly after dark, appalled the crews of other vessels, who saw it rapidly approaching in spite of adverse wind and tide."

The steam-powered paddle-wheeler made the trip from New York to Albany in twenty-eight hours and forty-five minutes. Thanks to Fulton and his satanic contraption, shippers and passengers were no longer completely at the mercy of the river sprites. No longer did passengers and cargo need to loll around waiting for the tide to turn or for a wind to come up. Now it was possible for boats to journey up and down the river on regular schedules. For economy, reliability and convenience, the steamboat was as great an improvement over sail as the automobile was to be over the horse and buggy.

As with any leap in technology, however, the steamboat had its drawbacks. Soot from the smokestacks coated everything. Boilers had a nasty habit of blowing up. It was a cool traveler who could walk up the gangway at the start of a voyage and not wonder whether the forthcoming trip might end prematurely in a blast of steam, fire and flying metal.

Nor were steamboats immune to the river's tricky currents and sudden storms. A cocky captain might strut the bridge, proud of his engine's ability to conquer the Hudson's calms and its contrary currents. But gales and churning seas could still turn a pleasant voyage into a perfect misery and send stout vessels to the bottom. Even today, the river claims more than its share of victims, despite modern engines that generate vastly more power and speed than Robert Fulton ever imagined.

Diego, thankfully, was in no hurry to put us at risk. He was a cautious teacher as well as a patient one, and during those Sunday morning classes, the river was more of a playground than a battleground. But we had our share of blustery mornings, when the wind kicked up whitecaps and heeled us far over. Then we'd white-knuckle the safety lines and watch the water rushing by just inches from where we braced our feet on the lee rail.

But in Diego's eyes, every experience was a teaching opportunity. Was the wind too strong? He showed us how to minimize its impact, either by easing out the sails to "dump" some wind or by "reefing": lowering the sail part way. Were we brought to a standstill by the tidal current? Diego made that a lesson, too. And when things got really nasty—the wind too strong, the waves too high—and the rest of us were hanging on for dear life, he'd calmly take the tiller and head us back to the marina.

Diego was a solid, reassuring presence. As long as he was with me in the cockpit, I had no doubt that I could eventually manage this sailing business. With each new class, each new experience, my confidence grew, and by the middle of my second season with Diego, I was feeling pretty sure that I could even handle a boat on my own.

That's when the trouble started.

That's when, God help me, I began to hear a seductive voice whispering in my ear. "Oh, yes," said the voice, "you can do this. No problem. But wouldn't it be great to be doing it in your own boat?"

# 4

# FOLLY

*"Nobody Needs a Boat."*
                    *—Diego Carr*

"Buy a sailboat? Are you crazy?"
    "Go for it!"
    "Don't you have enough problems?"
    "Hey, life is short. Do it while you can."
    The advice I heard from other people was as contradictory as the arguments that swirled around in my own brain. Part of me knew it was a loony idea. Even if I could afford it, how could I possibly justify spending money on something so frivolous? I was still paying the ransom for my son's college education. Our Chevy Nova was dying of old age and would soon need to be replaced. And what about the house? It badly needed a coat of paint and a new roof. If I didn't do something soon the neighbors would have me in court for dragging down property values.
    But it wasn't just the money that kept me from taking the leap. It was also the hassles that I kept hearing came with boats: the electrical repairs, the motor repairs, the cleaning and waxing and painting in spring; the hauling and scraping in the fall, and on and on, an endless litany. No, buying a boat was about the dumbest thing anybody could do. And yet . . .
    Despite all the sensible arguments against it, I could not ignore the seductive images that teased my imagination: the sun-bright seascapes, the dancing waves, the sweet breezes.
    Oh, they were clever, those folks at the Great Hudson Sailing Center. They knew from the beginning that this

would happen. I saw it clearly now. They had planned the whole thing. The classes were only the bait. Get a sucker out on the water a few times and you could bet your fiberglass bottom that he'd soon start seeing himself at the tiller of his own boat. Why else would they include that sneaky little footnote in their brochure:

> Graduates of the course will receive a 10% discount on the purchase of any boat.

My first thought was: Hey, good deal! My second thought was: Yeah, right. Ten percent off a bucket of money still leaves a bucket of money.

Yet that cunning little come-on worked its magic. After only a few lessons I was hooked. And now here I was, forever daydreaming about how I might/could/maybe/possibly someday find myself flying along on a fair breeze in my very own sweet sloop.

"What about that one there?" I asked Diego as we glided over Haverstraw Bay one Sunday morning. I had my eye on a pretty little sailboat that was gliding over the waves off our port side. It had a small cabin, a nice lift to the bow and graceful lines, and it looked about the right size for me: big enough to be comfortable but not so big that I couldn't single-hand it. "How much would something like that go for?" I asked.

No harm in asking, right? Just out of curiosity.

Diego shrugged. "It depends."

"Hmm," I said vaguely, wondering why he was being vague. Was it bad manners to ask the price of a boat? Was it a case of, If you have to ask you can't afford it? Or was he playing the coy salesman, refusing to be pinned down while keeping the negotiations open?

But I persisted. "Well, what would be, you know, sort of ball park?"

"Hard to say. So many factors come into it: age of the

boat, what condition she's in, how many extras are included, how eager the owner is to sell."

"Well, how about a boat like that one over there?"

"New? Maybe eighteen, twenty thousand. Twenty-five with all the bells and whistles."

"Hmm." I wanted to sound as if it didn't matter, but inwardly I groaned. Even stripped down, such a thing was well beyond my pocketbook.

"But forget buying a new one," Diego continued. "Why waste your money? There are all kinds of used boats you can get cheap."

"But then aren't you just buying someone else's problems? I mean, why would someone sell a boat if it didn't have problems?"

"Oh, people sell for all kinds of reasons. They want something bigger. Or their family situation changes. It could be anything. What you want to do is hang around the marinas, check out the 'for sale' signs, talk to people. When you see something you like, make a ridiculous offer. You never know. The owner might be desperate and want to make a deal."

A new chord thrumbed in my brain. Something in an upper register. Sea Major? And it continued to reverberate long after my lesson was over: Make an offer. Make an offer. Hmmm . . .

My timing was good. When I finally got around to sailing, it was easier than ever for the average guy to own a boat. Not too many years earlier, only the wealthy few could afford to keep sailboats just for the fun of it.

There were exceptions. In the early 1800s, working men in port cities like Philadelphia, New York and Boston began using small workboats for racing or for just dawdling around on summer afternoons. But unless he was a waterman by trade, the average person was unlikely to ever experience the enchantment of steering his own boat in a brisk breeze, with the wind in his hair and the waves tossing rainbows off his bow.

Such pleasures were reserved for royalty, merchants and business tycoons who had both the time and money to indulge their passion. It was a king, no less, who staged one of the earliest recorded yacht races: England's Charles II, who commanded a 49-foot Dutch-built yacht in a race against his brother, the Duke of York, in the late 1600s. Not long afterwards, in 1720, one of the first yacht clubs was founded: the Water Club of Cork Harbour, Ireland.

The first American yacht association was formed by a group of rich rowing enthusiasts in Detroit in 1839. But it was the founding of the New York Yacht Club in 1844 that gave yachting its first big boost in America. The club's founding fathers—kings of finance, steel, railroads and retail—were as fiercely competitive at play as they were in business and they pushed yacht designers and builders to create ever bigger and faster racing craft.

In 1851, invited to compete against a fleet of British boats, the club sent its sleek schooner-rigged yacht AMERICA across the Atlantic to meet the challenge. She won a decisive victory and was awarded what became the world's preeminent yachting trophy, the "hundred guinea cup" known forever after as the *America's Cup*.

Widely covered in the press, that first international race stirred patriotic fervor back home and excited enthusiasm for sport sailing in shore-side communities from Boston to New Orleans. Merchants and laborers, watermen and clerks took to racing in all kinds of small boats, from single-sail catboats in Massachusetts to log canoes in the Chesapeake and feisty little "tuckups" on Delaware Bay. And when, every few years, another British or Canadian club sought to regain the *America's Cup*, the well-publicized contests brought fresh bursts of enthusiasm for the sport.

By the 1880s, it seemed that every harbor, large and small, boasted its own yacht club. The tycoons still tended to hog all the attention, with their luxury yachts and professional skippers and crew. But by now they were far outnumbered by sailors of more modest means: determined amateurs who converted fishing boats and pilot cutters into cruising yachts and set off on long-distance seat-of-the-pants voyages to distant ports. Published accounts of their adventures created whole new generations of armchair adventurers and Sunday sailors.

At the same time, amateur racing became more tightly organized. The casual pickup races of old gave way to formal competitions, with rules set and boat sizes regulated to even the odds among the contestants. These one-design racing boats were soon being mass-produced, and as costs came down, sailing became more accessible than ever to the general population. Even during the economic slump that followed the First World War, yachting and recreational boating kept growing in popularity. By 1930, an estimated one-and-a-half million pleasure boats were afloat in the United States.

In those fruitful years, the general shape and design of small boats continued to evolve. Designers worked to refine the ancient workboat hulls to make them more efficient for racing and more comfortable for cruising. Sail plans were adapted as well. The centuries-old gaff-rigged setup, which was powered by a single, large sail hung between an upper and a lower boom, began to lose favor to the more efficient Marconi or sloop rig: a large triangular mainsail aft balanced by a smaller triangular sail up front.

This new fore-and-aft rig had some definite advantages. For one thing, two smaller sails were easier to raise, lower and maneuver than was a single large sail. And the shorter mainsail boom on the sloop was easier and safer to handle than the long boom of the gaff-rigged boat. When a gaff-rigged boat heeled over, its long boom could too easily end up dragging in the water and pulling the boat over.

Even with these changes, though, sailing still remained a relatively expensive pursuit for the average man and woman. Wooden boats, even mass-produced ones, were expensive to build. They required long hours of labor and the close attention of highly skilled craftsmen. Designers, seeking to bring costs down, experimented with hulls made of aluminum, steel and even concrete.

The breakthrough came with the introduction of a revolutionary new material: fiberglass. Developed during World War II for airplane wings, fiberglass laminates began to be used for boat building in the 1950s. Layers of fiberglass cloth and mat resins were applied over standard molds. Scores, even hundreds of boats could be built from the same mold. Costs fell, especially the cost of maintenance, and as the post-war economy boomed, sales soared. By 1970, fiberglass had replaced wooden hulls in nearly all American boat building.

At the same time, automobiles and boat trailers became more affordable, which meant that even people who lived far from the water could enjoy boating. The price of inboard and outboard engines also came down.

All these factors contributed to the explosive growth of boating as a sport and a way of life. By 1961 the number of powerboats and sailboats registered in the United States had risen to over seven million, and in the decades that followed, the number only increased. By 1996 there were more than 16 million pleasure boats scooting around on America's waterways.

That was about the time I started thinking about getting a boat of my own. And by then there were plenty of old boats to choose from: boats had been around for years; boats whose owners were just waiting for someone like me to come by and "make an offer."

\*　　\*　　\*

The good news was that the idea of owning a boat didn't scare me the way it would have a year or two earlier. The bad news was that the idea of owning a boat didn't scare me the way it would have a year or two earlier.

Having graduated from beginner classes to intermediate, I now felt fairly confident at the tiller. I was still glad to have Diego on hand in case I got into trouble. But I was almost ready to go solo. I knew the basics of how to trim the sails to take the best advantage of the wind. I had learned the importance of thinking ahead. Among other things that meant shortening sail before the breeze got so strong it threatened to blow me over. And when I jibed—made a turn with the wind behind me—I knew I'd better control the boom as it came swinging over to the other side of the boat. If it came over too fast and hard the shock could damage the rigging. It could also smack someone in the head and knock them overboard. And that someone could be me.

Thinking ahead also meant giving myself plenty of time to stay clear of the commercial traffic that made the river such a lively place: tugs pulling strings of gravel barges from nearby quarries; other tugs pushing oil barges from New Jersey depots to tank farms and power plants up the river; enormous freighters carrying Nova Scotia gypsum upriver to a wallboard plant in Haverstraw. Weekend tour boats carried sightseers from New York City upriver to West Point. High-speed power boats raced up and down the Hudson at sixty miles an hour, roaring like rocket ships and leaving huge wakes.

The barges were a special worry. As Diego liked to point out, getting run down by one of those babies could ruin your whole day. At speed, a barge was unable to stop or turn in much less than a mile, so it made sense to stay well clear. And if I found myself in the channel in light wind, or with no wind at all, I'd better be sure the outboard was ready to kick in so I could get out of the way fast.

By now, too, I knew the basic rules of the road. I knew that when two boats were passing, the boat sailing on the starboard tack had the right of way, and that two boats approaching head-on were expected to pass portside to portside. I knew that sailboats had the right of way over motorboats, but that it was not always a good idea to insist on that right, especially if the craft bearing down on you was the size of a football stadium.

Meantime, what I wasn't learning on the water, I was picking up in the classroom. During the winter I signed up for an evening course in coastal navigation at a nearby high school. With sleet clicking its fingers on the windows and snow swirling around the street lamps outside, eight other students and I huddled in the library, where the owner of a local sailing school guided us through the mysteries of nautical charts and the tide-and-current tables.

Our instructor's name was Tim, and he began by asking each of us what we hoped to get out of the course. I talked about wanting to learn the skill toward the day when I'd have a boat of my own. Others were back to refresh skills that they once knew but had mostly forgotten. The best response, though, came from a guy named Bert: "I want to find out where I'm going, how to get there, and where I am when I get there."

What self-help guru would not welcome that eloquent formulation of the path to right living?

With charts of Long Island Sound and Block Island Sound spread out on the library tables in front of us, we were soon plotting fantasy voyages to places like Shelter Island and Martha's Vineyard, warming our winter-numbed brains with visions of sparkling summer afternoons: all blue water, white sails and the sun glittering off the wave tops.

That some of the other students already owned their own boats reawakened those twinges of envy I'd felt when I first walked out onto the marina docks amid those gorgeous yachts. But this time it was different. Back then, if someone had asked me whether I was a boat owner, I would have answered "I wish." These days I was more likely to answer, "Not yet." The seed of a foolish hope had taken root in my brain and each new class, each new conversation with boat owners was like fertilizer, helping the seed to grow.

"Manure, you mean," said my sensible voice.

"Shut up," I replied, and listened in while my fellow students regaled one another with stories of voyages they had taken in their boats. Who knew what useful tips I might pick up? Each anecdote, each new bit of knowledge would put me that much further ahead on that grand day when I would finally take the plunge.

Our textbook was the boater's bible, Elbert S. Maloney's *Piloting, Seamanship and Small Boat Handling*, called *Chapman* for short, in honor of its first author. From Charles F. Chapman and his successors we learned how to identify buoys, channel markers, lights, shoals and the hundreds of other symbols that appear on charts. We learned how to use the equations of time, speed and distance to plot our current position and to project our future course.

From another reference work, *Eldridge Tide and Pilot Book*, we learned how to make allowances for tidal currents. In maps and tables the book spelled out everything any East Coast sailor needed to know about local sea forces operating on any particular hour, day or season for any particular year.

Were you planning to sail down the Hudson and out into Long Island Sound? You needed to know when the tide turned at the Battery, at the lower end of Manhattan. That way, you could use the outgoing tide to carry you down the Hudson, then ride the incoming tide for your run up the East River and out into the Sound. And once you were out in the Sound's wide-open spaces, you could take advantage of the tide's ebb and flow to speed you on your way to Cape Cod, Nantucket, the world.

Navigation, I began to see, was a lot like the Catholic catechism that had been drilled into me in grade school. It had its own rules, its own rewards and punishments. If you followed the rules, you could be pretty sure of making a safe passage. Mistakes and miscalculations—the sins of navigation—could land you in purgatory: a missed harbor, your boat aground, your position unknown. Mortal sins could very well send you to hell: a collision in the night; your boat on the rocks or smashed to bits against a piling. Virtues and indulgences were the things you did right. A few prayers now and then wouldn't hurt, either.

That first navigation course was a revelation. From it came a new way of seeing. In the past, when I had stood on a shore and gazed out across an expanse of water, I saw mere scenery: water in its many moods, passing boats, shore birds. Maybe there was a pretty lighthouse nearby to lend the scene a human scale.

But scenery, I now learned, was only the surface of the picture. The navigation course showed me a new reality, a more complicated narrative.

Of course I had always known that lighthouses and buoys had good, practical reasons for being where they were: that they warned boatmen of dangerous shoals and headlands and obstructions. I knew perfectly well that they did not exist solely to prettify the painter's composition or the photographer's postcard view. Still, until I took Tim's course, I had never imagined the wealth of information that was imbedded in every coastal seascape.

Learn to read the flashing lights out in a bay and you could identify precisely which port or shoal or rocky headland you were observing. Since each light had its own distinctive sequence of colors and flashes, it was possible to tell them apart by identifying their colors, by timing the intervals between flashes, and then looking up the corresponding information in Eldridge or some other official handbook.

Buoys, too, were more than just anonymous tin cans strung along the edge of a channel. Each had a distinctive shape, color and number that correlated to a mark on the chart. And each conveyed its own message to the navigator. In most North American waters, for instance, sailors can expect that when they are returning to port from the sea they will find red-painted buoys marking the right-hand side of the channel. "Red Right Returning" was the usual formula for remembering that rule. Green buoys, in turn, usually marked the left side of a channel.

I learned that lighthouses and other shore markers not only indicate headlands and shoals; they could also be used as bearing markers to help you check your direction and distance traveled. With a little trigonometry you could even calculate your distance from a particular lighthouse, since the height of each lighthouse was marked on charts and in official handbooks.

I learned, too, that understanding the lights on boats would be an essential skill if I ever found myself sailing at night. For now, I could practice by watching the river at night from the shore. Was that a green light I saw moving across the water? I was seeing the boat's starboard side. A red light meant I was seeing its port side. If I saw red and green together, the boat was coming toward me. A white light at water level meant I was seeing a boat's stern.

And what about that tug churning up the river, the one that could be heard rumbling like a slow-moving freight train on a quiet night? Was she towing a string of barges? The sequence of lights on her mast could tell me, as could the lights on the barges that the tug might be pushing or pulling. Given such knowledge, a skipper would know whether it was safe to pass astern of the tug, or whether he might be dismasted or even decapitated by a tow cable. It was a gruesome thought, but that was exactly what had happened to the captain of a cabin cruiser on Long Island Sound a few years earlier.

To my new eyes, the coastal waters were no longer an aimless expanse, but a carefully ordered landscape, a book to be read and studied. It was as if a curtain had been drawn aside, revealing an entirely new view of the world.

Most of all, Tim's course taught me just how little I knew and how much more there always was to learn, whether about boats or charts, sailing techniques or weather. With each class I became more intrigued with the complexities of my new endeavor. I was beginning to realize that sailing was an endless process of education and discovery. The more you learned the more there was to learn. And that was one of the things that made sailing so fascinating, so engaging of both my brain and my senses.

I couldn't get enough of it. In the summer, when I wasn't taking classes, I tried my skills in a rented day sailer: a quick little seventeen- or eighteen-footer. And once, while Ellen and I were vacationing on Cape Ann, north of Boston, I rented a nifty little Rhodes 19 and dared the ocean itself.

Ellen stayed ashore. She had never shared my enthusiasm for the joys of a cramped cockpit, a heeling wind and rolling seas. As I set off in late morning she chose the traditional role of the sailor's wife: waiting by the window of our room, a book in her hand, a cold glass of lemonade at her elbow, and hope in her heart for her husband's safe return.

I had read enough accounts of adventures at sea to know that out on the ocean I could expect a very different kind of sailing from what I was used to on the Hudson. There the hills and shoreline gave at least some protection from the wind and kept the waves to manageable heights. At sea I'd have no such protection and nowhere to run if things went bad. Out there the winds had countless unobstructed miles to do their work. They could pile waves to daunting heights and turn the biggest ships into matchsticks. Every sea story worth its salt included raging storms, huge rogue waves, masts broken, men overboard.

One circumnavigator advised those who would follow in his path to keep a flashlight secured to the cabin floor. "That way, when your boat goes belly-up in heavy seas at night you'll be able to find your light easily."

Belly-up? In the middle of the ocean? In the dark? Yikes!

But as I set out on that fine August morning, any such dire fate seemed highly unlikely. The sun was bright and a light northerly breeze was rippling the surface of the bay, offering the promise of good sailing.

Well swabbed in sunscreen and covered up in a wide-brimmed hat and long-sleeved shirt, I bicycled over to the rental office. A towheaded teenager behind the counter ran my credit card through the machine, then led me out to the stone quay where the boats were tied up. I stepped down into my assigned vessel, stowed my lunch bag and water bottle in the cuddy and hoisted the main and jib. The boy cast off the lines, gave me a push with his bare foot, and watched as I hardened up the sails and let the breeze carry me past the breakwater and out into Sandy Bay.

With my hat pulled down over my eyes, I steered east toward the mouth of the little bay, where the ocean began. Soon I was past the headland, and there for the first time I felt the surge of the sea, its swells rising and falling beneath me, picking me up and easing me down, nudging me along in an exhilarating coital rhythm.

I went with the flow. The open sea and the steady breeze were intoxicating, and I had all the time in the world. Ellen wasn't expecting me back for hours.

Seeing the surf crashing over an offshore rock ledge, I headed over to investigate, hoping to see a seal or two. I got as close to the rocks as I dared but saw no signs of life. Veering away, I headed downwind and down current, aiming toward a set of twin lighthouses perched on a distant island. On shore I could see people standing on the rocks and lying on the beaches, and I was pleased to know that my little boat and I were part of the picture-postcard view for anyone gazing out to sea. I thought of that little boy standing on the shore of Lake Michigan all those years ago, watching the distant sails and daydreaming about voyages over the horizon, and now here I was, doing just that. I couldn't help but grin at my good fortune.

I sailed on and on, letting the sea surge and the wind carry me along. But the island with its twin lights did not seem to get any closer and meantime the sun was getting higher and hotter, and when I looked back and saw the headland at Sandy Bay far behind me I realized that I had come much further than I had thought. I had already devoured my sandwich and apple and my water was half gone. I also needed to allow time for the trip back. Although I was still well short of my goal, I knew it would be foolish to press on.

Reluctantly I turned the boat around—and only then realized that I might be in trouble. The current was against me and the wind was definitely lighter than it had been an hour earlier. Getting back to the dock was not going to be easy. For a while I wondered if it would even be possible. I had no idea how the currents ran out here, or whether they would reverse themselves with the changing tide, as they did on the Hudson. If the wind died completely I might just end up being carried out to sea. What then? Would anyone come looking for me? Would they be able to find me before dark, a tiny sail on a vast ocean?

A canoe paddle lay in the bottom of the boat. But would it do any good against the current? Meanwhile, the wind continued to fall off and the August sun was getting hotter by the minute. What if . . . ?

Wiping sweat from my forehead, concentrating hard, I played the sails and the tiller to grab every whiff of wind.

Luckily there was just enough of it to counter the current, and as I checked my progress against the shoreline I was relieved to see that I was making headway, however slowly.

It was mid-afternoon before I reached the headland and another half hour before I reached the breakwater at the inner harbor. By then the sea was flat calm and I had to paddle the last hundred yards to the dock.

I was exhausted and dazed from the sun glare when I finally tossed the dockline to the barefoot boy.

He took the line and cleated it off. "I didn't know where you were," he said. He sounded miffed. Apparently I had violated the rental guidelines by sailing past the headland and out of sight. Had I been swept away by the current the kid would have been in a bad spot: boat lost; customer lost. On the evening news he would have been known as "the last person to see the victim alive." It wouldn't look good on his college applications.

I shrugged an apology. "I guess I got carried away." I climbed out of the boat and onto the quay and changed the subject. "Nice little boat. Handles really well."

It was a funny thing: in just those few hours on the water the rhythm of the sea had gotten into my blood. The pavement seemed to roll under my feet as I walked back into town. But despite my lurching gait I felt both invigorated and very pleased with myself. With patience and some skill I had wriggled my way out of a difficult situation. I couldn't stop smiling at my triumph. I was still smiling when I walked into our room.

Ellen looked up from her book. "Have a good time?"

"Wonderful!"

"How come you're so late? I was getting worried."

I shrugged, tried to sound casual. "Oh, the wind dropped. It took a little while to get back in, that's all. No big deal."

As I chugged down a big glass of water, I reined in my

impulse to tell her the whole story. I had sense enough to realize it was not the kind of tale guaranteed to relieve her anxieties the next time I sailed off into the unknown. The exciting parts had happened because I'd been careless: had gone out too far; had misjudged the currents. The less said about that the better. Instead, I recounted the great ride I'd had at the start: the exhilaration of being carried along by the sea surge; my delight at being able to maneuver through the tricky harbor currents. "It was fabulous!" I concluded.

"My hero!" Ellen said and got up to give me a kiss. "Now can we go to dinner?"

If I was disappointed by Ellen's lack of enthusiasm it was only because I had forgotten the truism that sea stories, like golf and fishing stories, tend to be far more interesting to the participants than to those who stand and wait. It was also true that, measured against the great sagas of the sea, my little holiday adventure was a trifle, no more epical in scale or drama than an afternoon outing on a rowing pond.

And yet, compared to the desk-bound routine of my daily life, that first sea voyage was utterly thrilling. When else did I feel that adrenaline surge, that level of concentration and focus, that sense of being connected to the elemental heart of things?

My confidence, too, had gotten a boost. I had handled that little boat well in tricky conditions and now, far from being scared off, I found myself hungry for more. I felt more ready and more eager than ever to take the next step: to have a boat of my own.

I couldn't wait. I could imagine it so easily. Owning a boat, I'd be free to sail whenever I had a few hours to spare. Every weekend would be a vacation. And I could get to know a boat and master it in a way that I could not do when jumping from one rental to another.

I yearned. I daydreamed. But still I held off. Money was no less a problem than before; I was still in no position to plunk down thousands of dollars for a mere plaything—a toy, for God's sake.

I was troubled, too, by the nagging voice of conscience. It whispered in my ear that owning a boat was not only self-indulgent but morally corrupt. I could almost smell the incense and hear the muffled voice of the priest in the confessionals of my childhood. How could I possibly justify such hedonism when so many people in the world suffered from starvation, war, violence and the whole terrible litany of human degradation and injustice? If and when I had extra money, shouldn't I send it to Amnesty International and the Fellowship of Reconciliation and Greenpeace and Save the Children? That would be the right thing to do.

But another voice struggled to be heard as well. "Lighten up!" it said. "Stop being such a goody-goody. You do your bit. You send your donations. You protest. You sit on social service boards. Do you really imagine that your little frivolous indulgence will take food out of a child's mouth or keep someone in a foreign prison a few days longer? This is also your life, right here, right now. You don't get another chance. Live it while you can."

I couldn't help it. I loved that sweet, rationalizing, self-justifying voice the best. In the duet of conflicting impulses, it sang the most melodiously in my ear.

Anyway, at bottom I did not believe that my fascination with boats was entirely frivolous. To discover new ways of seeing the world, to savor Nature's abundant gifts, to feel connected to the primal elements of wind and water and weather, and through them to feel my spirit and my imagination enriched and strengthened—these were far from being trivial pursuits. They were as essential to my spirit as eating and breathing.

\*       \*       \*

Wind and water. Sails and keel. Need and desire. Conscience and pleasure. In life as in sailing, the trick was to keep the opposing forces in balance.

At least those were the thoughts rattling around in my brain in the weeks following my splendid summer adventure. And they were still tossing and tumbling around in there, like laundry in a dryer, on the day that I saw her: the boat of my dreams.

It was early October. I had driven over to a nearby chandlery during my lunch hour to buy foul-weather boots. Having signed up with Diego for a late-season coastal-cruising class, I wanted to be prepared for wet weather and slippery decks.

I found the boots I wanted, and as I dug out my credit card and waited while the sales clerk wrote up my receipt, I asked off-handedly if he had any boats for sale. I wasn't really ready to buy, but I figured there was no harm in asking.

"Maybe," he said. "What are you looking for?"

"Oh, nothing too big. A nineteen- or twenty-footer, say."

"We got a couple in that range. Wanna take a look?"

I shrugged. "Sure. Why not."

The minute I saw her I was smitten. Her name was MAR-GOT, she was twenty feet long and she had just come on the market.

Tethered to the end of a dock, bobbing gently on her lines, MARGOT wasn't exactly sleek and graceful. She was a little too short for that, a little too broad abeam. But overall she was a pretty sloop and from the look of her, she had been loved and well cared for. Her mast shone with that milky gray light of polished aluminum, her mainsail was flaked neatly over the boom. The halyards and sheets were neatly coiled, the compass and depth sounder appeared brand new. The varnish on the graceful swan's-neck tiller gleamed warmly.

With approval I noticed that the jib was fitted to a roller-furling rig, a kind of window-shade arrangement that allowed the skipper to let out the foresail or roll it up by haul-ing on a line from the cockpit. Without roller-furling, some-one had to climb out onto the foredeck to raise or douse the sail. And since I expected to be doing most of my sailing single-handed, roller furling was a must.

Stepping down into the cockpit, I saw that it was roomy enough to accommodate myself and one or two guests. I pushed back the hatch cover and, bending almost double, I went down the single step into the cabin. It was tiny and I had to squat on my heels to keep from bumping my head on the ceiling. But four bunks were squeezed in down there, a V-berth up front and two singles tucked in the stern, under the cockpit seats. Large windows made the cabin bright and cheery even on this overcast day, and there were various cozy conveniences, including a small sink, a freezer box and a little table. A porta-potty was hidden up front, under a drop board in the V-berth.

I lifted a cushion. It was soggy underneath. Was there a leak somewhere, or was the dampness only from condensa-tion? I lifted a floorboard and saw that the bilge was per-fectly dry. So probably nothing leaked.

Stepping back up into the cockpit, I unfolded myself and looked over the topsides once more. Everything I saw was encouraging: the roller furling, the neatly flaked mainsail, the general good order of things. I also liked the fact that the boat had a fixed keel rather than a centerboard.

Centerboard boats certainly had advantages. With the board up you could go poking into shallow bays and estu-aries where a keelboat would run aground. (I loved the term for this kind of exploring: "gunkholing," it was called, evok-ing lazy afternoons of idle wandering and quiet evenings at anchor in marshy backwaters.)

Small centerboard boats could also be mounted on trail-ers for trips to more distant cruising grounds. And when the season was over, you could save yourself a bundle in storage fees by keeping the trailer-mounted boat in your driveway.

But centerboards worried me. For one thing, I harbored a profound mistrust of any boat that had a large hole in the bottom. Yes, I knew that centerboards were stowed in waterproof housings; still, on some primal level, my mind simply refused to accept that this was a good idea.

I had other reservations as well. You lifted a centerboard by cranking up a cable onto a drum, using a winch handle. If the cable broke or came off its drum—as happened once when I was sailing on a friend's boat—you could not get the board back up without hauling the boat out of the water. And if you left it at its mooring with the board dangling in the turning current or, worse, if it got stuck on a shallow bottom when the tide went out, the board could be wrenched back and forth until it either opened a seam in the hull or was torn off the single swivel pin that held it in place. Who wanted to worry about stuff like that? Enough things could go wrong with a boat. Why go looking for trouble?

Besides, my vision for my sailing future included deepwater voyages: down the coast to Chesapeake Bay, perhaps, or out through Long Island Sound to Martha's Vineyard. At sea I'd want a heavy keel to keep my boat upright. Anyway, with a heavy keel under you the ride felt a whole lot more stable than in a centerboard board, and I knew Ellen would like that—if and when I could persuade her to come out with me.

From everything I could see, MARGOT filled all my requirements.

"Nice boat," I told the clerk as I stepped up back up onto the dock. "How come she's for sale?"

It turned out that the owner, a guy in his seventies, had developed a bad case of arthritis. Sailing a sloop singlehanded had become too difficult for him. He was looking for something easier to sail, maybe a single-sailed catboat. He was asking $3000 for MARGOT but would probably take $2500, maybe even less.

"Really?" I was surprised by the low price, and I'm afraid I let it show—a poor negotiating tactic.

"Yeah. He's anxious to sell before he has to haul her out and store her for the winter."

"Is the motor included?"

"No, he wants to keep it for his next boat. But we could find you a motor, no problem. There are plenty of used ones around."

"How much would that be?"

"Oh, four or five hundred bucks."

I was getting more excited by the minute. All along I had thought I'd have to pay thousands more for a boat; I'd have to wait years before I could afford one. Suddenly the dream seemed possible, and a lot sooner than I'd expected. It might even happen now! Today!

All the way back to the office I thought about MARGOT. I didn't drive into a ditch so I must have seen the road in front of me. But in my mind's eye I saw only that pretty little boat, with me at the helm, the wind in my face, the water rushing past, the whole world opened before me.

Could I make it happen? I didn't have extra cash in the bank, but if I could pay in installments. . . . No, that wouldn't work. I was just barely keeping up with our bills as it was. Besides, it wasn't just the boat I'd have to pay for. I'd need money for a used motor, money for winter hauling and storage fees, money for summer docking fees. How much was I looking at here? I had no idea. I needed some answers.

Back at the office I ignored the work on my desk, phoned Information, and got the number for Petersen's, one of my local boatyards.

The woman who answered the phone was pleasant, helpful, and full of information. But her news was not good. Even if I could get the purchase price down to $2500, I'd still have to spend at least double that to cover all the other costs. And then there was all the time and effort that I'd need to spend just to maintain the thing: scraping and painting the bottom in spring, waxing and polishing the hull, keeping the sails clean and the motor running.

Given all I knew, did I really want to make the leap? Did I really need a boat?

Diego, as always, set me straight.

It was a cool evening in mid-October and we were anchored in a quiet harbor on Long Island's North Shore. With two other students, I had spent the day in Diego's fine old 32-foot CONSUELA, practicing the art and science of coastal navigation. Having studied the tide and current tables, we had left Haverstraw that morning on the outgoing tide. Sailing down the Hudson, we had rounded lower Manhattan just in time to catch the incoming tide, which helped carry us up the East River and out into Long Island Sound, where we had practiced matching what we saw on the water with what was depicted on the charts: buoys, islands, lights and landmarks.

It had been a long day, and now, following a hearty dinner in the galley, we sat in the cockpit sipping beers, talking quietly and admiring the nighttime view of harbor lights and a star-filled sky. Bundled up in my down jacket and wool cap, my feet nice and toasty inside my new foul-weather boots, I was feeling mellow and meditative, and I soon fell to mulling over my boat-buying dilemma.

"The problem is," I said, "I'm having a hard time justifying it to myself. From everything I hear boats are just really impractical. They're one headache after another. I mean, do I really need that?"

Diego's cigarette glowed in the darkness as he took a drag. "Look, nobody *needs* a boat," he replied reasonably. "You need a roof over your head. You need a car. You need food on the table and clothes on your back. But nobody needs a boat. And if you're worried about being practical, forget boats. There's nothing practical about them. You get a boat because you want one. That's the only reason."

"Mmm," I said. I knew he was right. Did I need a boat? Of course not. Did I want one? As I sat there beneath the stars and felt the gentle rocking of the boat beneath me and heard the quiet voices of my companions as they, too, savored the beautiful night, I knew the answer as clearly as I had ever known anything.

# 5

# TAKING THE LEAP

*"Patience is bitter, but its fruits are sweet."*
*—Jean Jacques Rousseau*

I wondered: Was there a twelve-step program for boat addicts, a place where people sat around in a circle and tried to talk through their sickness? I could just imagine the conversation:

"Hi, my name is Tom and I'm a junkie."

"Cool! I always wanted a Chinese yacht."

"How big is she?"

"How does she handle?"

At this point the therapist would surely intervene: "Wait a minute, guys, I think Tom means he's addicted."

If such a program did exist, I certainly would have qualified for admission. I even had enablers to egg me on: Ellen and our son, Jesse. They wanted me to be happy, bless their hearts. Instead of trying to bring me to my senses, they encouraged my lunatic craving.

"Do it," said Jess, and his was a powerful endorsement. What father does not wish to dare bold deeds and so become a hero in his son's eyes? Only later did it occur to me that the lad might have had ulterior motives: Given my example, who knew what foolishness he might feel free to pursue?

The big surprise was Ellen's reaction when she learned of my near indiscretion with MARGOT. My passion for that pert little boat had been cooled as effectively as a cold shower by my phone conversation with the woman at Petersen's. Her recitation of the various costs I would incur had left me no choice. There was simply no way I could afford to make the leap. I would just have to wait a little longer.

Nobly I had turned my back on MARGOT that afternoon. But I was grieved by the loss, and when I came home that evening Ellen took one look and knew something was wrong.

"What happened?" she asked. "Don't tell me. You got fired."

"No."

"Laid off?"

"No, no. Nothing like that."

"What then? Something must have happened. You look awful."

"Really, it's okay. Everything's fine. It doesn't matter. It's just . . . Aw, hell."

I confessed everything then. About falling in love. About feeling oh-so-tempted. About nearly giving in to temptation, but then turning away because I remembered where my true loyalties lay: with my family, whose love I cherished and whose well-being was my first priority.

It was a shabby performance, rank with false nobility. What I secretly hoped was that she would be so impressed with my candor and self-sacrifice that she'd urge me to reconsider: "Oh, honey, if it means so much to you, why not just call the bank and take out a loan? I'm sure we could manage the payments. I can always get another job. And no, don't worry about Jesse and college. He'd be just as happy bagging groceries for the rest of his life. The leaky roof? Don't worry about it. It's not raining today anyway."

But of course she said no such thing. Her effort at bucking up my spirits consisted of agreeing with my decision to forego MARGOT's expensive charms.

"It's still too soon," she said.

My spirits sank even lower.

But then a remarkable thing happened. As I sat crestfallen at the kitchen table, my pathetic confession lying between us like something our aging and incontinent dog had left on the rug, my beloved wife reached out a sympathetic hand. "It will happen," she told me. "You'll know when it's right."

Could it be? By doing the responsible thing, by keeping

my passion in check, I had inadvertently restored her faith in me. Ellen now could see that her addle-brained husband was not about to go running off with the first pretty thing that came along.

This was good. Although I had failed to gain an immediate, "sure, go ahead, dear," I apparently had won points in the confidence department, and that would certainly be useful in the future, when the real thing came along.

One benefit turned up next summer on my fiftieth birthday, when Ellen decided my party should have a nautical theme.

"Are you sure?" I cautioned. "This boat stuff is tricky. It could get out of hand. Once you start encouraging a guy's impulses, there's no telling where it might lead. Babies. A boat in the driveway."

She smiled benignly. "It didn't work out so badly last time."

"Last time?"

"Jesse."

"Ah."

Looking back, it seems absurd that I dreaded the arrival of a birthday with so few years attached to it. At the time, though, the numbers seemed appalling. Of the two digits, one was a five and the other was a very large zero. Combined, they bore no relation whatever to the guy whose shoes I walked in every day. That guy had just graduated from high school. My only consolation was that I did not feel old and decrepit, and that alone was cause for celebration.

Celebrating was exactly what we had in mind that Sunday when my little family and I were joined by a dozen or so friends and relatives for an afternoon excursion up the Hudson. Our vessel was the COMMANDER, an ornate, turn-of-the-century tour boat fitted with a mock paddlewheel at her stern. As she carried us up the river through the Highlands, we sipped champagne from plastic glasses while strolling her open-air top deck and gazing at the stunning landscape of forest-clad mountains that rose on either side.

A potluck lunch in the lounge was followed by cake and

a hearty round of "Happy Birthday." Then came the gifts, and I was happy to see that the nautical theme prevailed. From Ellen I received a wide-brimmed Tilly hat, complete with a chin strap to keep the thing on my head during the gales I would surely face at sea. From a couple who were long-time friends came a rigging knife and a safety whistle, complete with properly nautical lanyards, to be tied to my clothing for safety. Steve, my boat-owning brother-in-law, presented me with a subscription to a glossy sailing magazine. There was also a set of charts of the lower Hudson River and New York Harbor, as well as a ship's log, ready to be filled in with details of my forthcoming voyages.

Best of all, I was now the happy recipient of not one but two copies of the latest edition of *Chapman*. One, bound in red buckram, came from the estimable Jess; he must have saved for months to pay for it. And in case anyone thought that having two copies was redundant, I was quick to disabuse them. "This is great!" I enthused. "I'll have one copy for the house and one for the boat."

"You've got a boat?" asked friend Marji, surprised.

"Not yet. But when I do, I'll be ready."

After that there was no going back. With my aspirations now known to one and all, could I do any less than take the next step? I had the skill. I had the books, the charts and all the gear I needed. Could a boat be far behind?

And if I did not have the money just yet, well, that was really a blessing in disguise. It gave me time to decide just what kind of boat was right for me. It forced me to take the time to do proper research, so that by the end of that summer I knew far more about boats than I did when I met MARGOT.

True, there were times when the impatient adolescent would shove aside the stolid householder and throw a tantrum. During a casual stroll through a marina, I'd find myself carried away by a mad, irrational lust for some beautiful boat or other. Then, for a crazed few hours, all my good intentions would vanish as I schemed and connived to come up with the money.

But in the end, with Ellen's help, I'd invariably came to my senses and the fever would subside. At such times I'd find myself awed, even humbled by Ellen's willingness to stick with me through my periodic bouts of insanity. It was hard on her, but she was learning what the wives of sailors have known from earliest times: that with men and boats, insanity is always part of the equation.

That's why, when the day finally came that I found exactly the right boat, at exactly the right time and exactly the right price, neither of us was quite ready to believe it. Was it really possible that my dream might come true? Or was I fooling myself again?

An afternoon ramble was all I had in mind on that mild Sunday afternoon in the middle of March: a chance for the two of us to spend some time together before the start of another busy week. We had driven to Piermont, a village a few miles down river from our Nyack home. While Ellen looked into shop windows, admiring the season's new fashions and crafts, my eyes were on the Hudson, which was just visible beyond the village park. I was hoping to catch a sight of a sail or two, but the river was empty. It was still too early in the season, but not by much. The air was balmy and there was a sweet, soggy breeze off the water.

"Coffee?" I suggested as we strolled toward the Community Market.

"Just coffee?" She raised an amused eyebrow.

"Well, maybe a scone, too."

"How did I guess?"

I held the door as she stepped into the market, which was a combination bakery and gourmet food mart, with a nice selection of take-out coffees and teas. I was about to follow her inside when I caught sight of an ad taped to the front window. It brought me to a dead stop.

The window served as the community bulletin board, a free-form collage of cards and fliers that advertised everything from apartment rentals and handyman services to Reiki therapy and cooking classes. Normally I barely glanced at the ads, but today one hand-made sign jumped out at me. It showed a precise, side-view drawing of a little sloop, sails raised. A list of specs was printed down one side. My heart did a little skip as I read the ad:

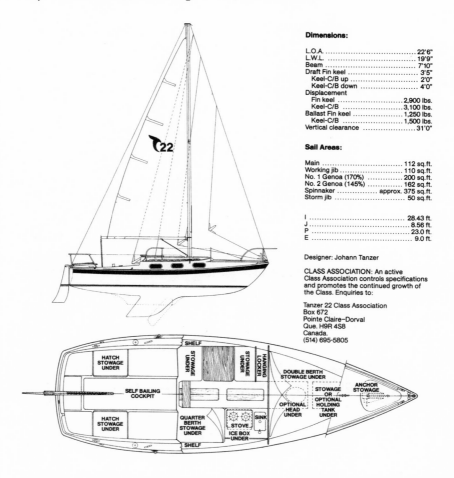

**Dimensions:**

| | |
|---|---|
| L.O.A. | 22'6" |
| L.W.L. | 19'9" |
| Beam | 7'10" |
| Draft Fin keel | 3'5" |
| Keel-C/B up | 2'0" |
| Keel-C/B down | 4'0" |
| Displacement | |
| Fin keel | 2,900 lbs. |
| Keel-C/B | 3,100 lbs. |
| Ballast Fin keel | 1,250 lbs. |
| Keel-C/B | 1,500 lbs. |
| Vertical clearance | 31'0" |

**Sail Areas:**

| | |
|---|---|
| Main | 112 sq.ft. |
| Working jib | 110 sq.ft. |
| No. 1 Genoa (170%) | 200 sq.ft. |
| No. 2 Genoa (145%) | 162 sq.ft. |
| Spinnaker | approx. 375 sq.ft. |
| Storm jib | 50 sq.ft. |

| | |
|---|---|
| I | 28.43 ft. |
| J | 8.56 ft. |
| P | 23.0 ft. |
| E | 9.0 ft. |

Designer: Johann Tanzer

CLASS ASSOCIATION: An active Class Association controls specifications and promotes the continued growth of the Class. Enquiries to:

Tanzer 22 Class Association
Box 672
Pointe Claire–Dorval
Que. H9R 4S8
Canada.
(514) 695-5805

For Sale: Beautiful mini-yacht. Large cockpit, sleeps four. Excellent single-handed day sailer with room and comfort for extended trips. FAST, STURDY. New bottom paint, waxed. Get in and go. Length 22'6". Beam 7'10". Fin keel. Three sails. Mercury outboard (8-horse).

My pulse was really clipping along now. This boat looked exactly like what I was after: keel rather than centerboard; small enough to manage single-handed, but with the graceful lines of a much larger boat. And the asking price of five thousand dollars was just about what I was prepared to pay.

Diego's words came back to me: "Make a ridiculous offer. You never know." These days, though, I could even manage the full price. Things had changed dramatically since I first began dreaming about buying a boat. I now had money in the bank. After years of picking away at my book in my spare time, I had finally finished the thing the previous autumn and sent it off to my agent. Just six weeks ago, a publisher had come through with a contract and an advance against future royalties. The amount I had already received would easily cover the cost of this boat.

Fighting to rein in my excitement, I stepped inside, borrowed pencil and paper from a clerk, and jotted down the phone number. *Calm down,* I told myself. *There's no point in getting all worked up. You don't even know if the boat is still available. There's no date on the ad. Who knows how long it's been posted there?*

The only way to find out was to call. I looked around for a phone. Then I caught myself. I had promised Ellen that we would spend this afternoon together. No work, no distractions. I would keep my word, wait until evening to call. If the boat was gone, too bad. There'd be others.

Getting a grip on myself, I tucked the phone number away in my shirt pocket and, keeping a calm demeanor, joined Ellen at the bakery counter. As if nothing had happened. As if my blood pressure were perfectly normal. As if the sun hadn't just peeked through the clouds.

"So what'll it be?" I asked her, studying the scones and muffins in the bakery case: "Blueberry or cranberry?"

"How about one of each?"

"Good idea."

\*    \*    \*

The drawing in the store window turned out to be a pale imitation of the real thing, as I discovered the next day when I had my first look at her. Bobbing at her mooring just off-shore, a few hundred yards downstream from the Tappan Zee Bridge, she looked like a puppy tugging at a leash, eager to be taken out for a run. Her gleaming white hull was accented with a rakish blue stripe, and the graceful lift of her bow and stern gave her a wonderfully jaunty profile. I liked her immediately.

The boat's owner—his name was Murdock—had invited me to meet him at a certain address on River Road, near where the boat was moored. From there he'd take me out to see her.

Lean and fit, and probably in his mid-thirties, Murdock sported a mane of curly red hair and an effulgent red beard. Fitted out with a kilt and a broadsword, he'd have looked as wild and warlike as any of the Scottish Highlanders from which he was nay doot descended. But his ready grin and lively blue eyes were anything but warlike, and as he led me over to a rubber dinghy and shoved us off from shore, he was both cheerful and chatty.

"She's really a sweet boat," he said as he rowed us over. "I was almost hoping no one would answer the ad. I hate to let her go."

"So why are you selling her?"

"If it was just me I'd hang on to her. She's great. But my kids are getting bigger and we need more room."

The boat's name was ECHO and the closer we got, the better she looked. She really didn't need a sales pitch. Just sitting there at her mooring, all pretty and pert, she was selling herself. As we climbed aboard, I saw nothing to alter my first impressions.

She was in immaculate shape. The teak drop boards of the cabin door and the teak handrails that ran along the

When I first saw ECHO tethered at her mooring just downstream from the Tappan Zee Bridge, it was love at first sight.

cabin top shone warmly in the mellow spring sunshine, and the hull and decks were spotless. She was twenty-five years old, twenty-two feet long, and had the usual amenities down below in the cabin: a fold-out table, banquet seats, a tiny sink, a porta-potty. There were berths for four, but as always with boats this size, unless the four were either really small or really close friends, four was a few too many to be comfortable. For me, though, this was no problem. When I thought of sailing I never envisioned doing it with a crowd.

Back on deck, I gave the boat a thorough eyeballing and went through my mental checklist. I saw nothing that seemed seriously wrong or out of place. The rigging looked sound, with no signs of corrosion at the turnbuckles that secured the shrouds to the deck, and with no apparent fraying of the shrouds themselves. The interior seemed dry and I detected no mildew odor. I did see a few spider-web cracks in the gelcoat, and the tiller handle needed a good coat of varnish. But none of these flaws were structural, and I found nothing amiss that might give me any bargaining leverage. Still, on general principles I made a stab at negotiating with braw Murdock. Would the laddie take $4500?

Nay, he would not. The price was five thousand, take it or leave it.

I nodded. Five thousand seemed fair. After all, even though the boat was twenty-five years old, it looked almost as good as new and came complete with all the essentials: sails, motor, battery. I was tempted to close the deal right then and there. But I forced myself to wait, to give myself time to think about it.

"I'll let you know tomorrow," I told Murdock after he had rowed us back to shore.

"That's fine," he said. "Talk to you then."

I told Ellen about the boat when I got home, and she gave me her full confidence. Whatever I decided would be okay with her.

"The money's there," she said. "You earned it. If the boat looks good to you, go ahead."

Still, as I lay in bed that night, I worried: Was I doing the right thing? Was I overlooking anything? Had I missed some major flaw? Was there a better boat out there somewhere, at a better price?

At bottom, though, I knew I had already made my decision.

The next morning I took a deep breath, picked up the phone, and told Murdock he had a deal. We arranged to meet again on the shore, and there, within sight of the boat, I handed him a check for the deposit. I promised the rest by the end of the week, when he'd have the bill of sale and the title ready and I'd have made the necessary arrangements on my end.

We shook hands and I walked back to my car a happy man—walked away, but kept glancing back over my shoulder at that pretty little boat out there on the river. I couldn't stop grinning. It was really going to happen. That boat would soon be mine.

# 6

# READY ABOUT

*". . . and tell me, wasn't that the best time,*
*that time when we were young at sea . . . ?"*
                                        *—Joseph Conrad*

Beginning with MARGOT and continuing through each of my later flirtations with an assortment of seductive little boats, one question had remained unresolved: Once I had a boat, where would I keep it?

Marinas were too expensive. I could park it on a trailer in the driveway, but how would I tow it unless I spent big bucks on a pickup or an SUV? Besides, if I had to drag a boat down to a launch ramp every time I wanted to sail, then had to get the thing into the water and raise the mast and mount the tiller and all the rest, I doubted I'd ever want to do much sailing.

The solution had turned up in what was, for me, a surprising place: the Nyack Boat Club.

Until I began sailing I had taken little notice of the place. True, I had often admired the charming Victorian clubhouse, with its gabled roofs, rambling side porches, and tree-shaded yard. And the location was spectacular: set on the crest of a bluff overlooking the Hudson. The porches and picnic grounds had wonderful views of the river and the Westchester hills across the way. From the gate at the top of the driveway you could see a long pier reaching out into the river. Beyond the pier, out in the river, a hundred or more sailboats were lined up in neat rows, bobbing at their moorings like a well-disciplined fleet of swans.

As inviting as the scene was, however, I had never before been tempted to step through the gate to see what else the club might have to offer. Becoming a club member had never been one of my life's aspirations. Even as a kid I had avoided group entanglements; instinctively I mistrusted the demands for conformity that seemed to be the price you paid for companionship. The Boy Scouts? Too authoritarian. Fraternities? I pledged one in college, but blew my chances by breaking out in a fit of giggles during the initiation ceremony. For my irreverence I was shown the door and told never to come back. Since then I had remained devoutly unaffiliated. No Kiwanis, no Elk, no Moose or Marmut had ever claimed my allegiance.

So I was surprised and a little nervous to find myself standing at the entrance to the boat club one sunny Sunday morning, contemplating the sign posted at the gate. "Private Property," it declared in bold letters; "Members Only." The message could not have been clearer: This was a bastion of privilege and exclusivity. Only the select few were to be admitted.

Until now that had been fine with me. If they wanted their privacy, they could have it. Why should I care? Nowadays, though, I saw things differently. Seduced by the sight of all those boats out in the river, I was ready to overlook my aversion to clubs and to the kind of snoots who joined them. After all, who knew what opportunities I might be missing? Why, there might be very nice people among the club's members. And some of them might even be looking for crew. I'd be crazy to let my prejudices get in the way of a chance to go sailing.

With that thought in mind, I strode blithely past the "Members Only" sign, through the gate and along the walkway that led past the clubhouse. Approaching the terrace out back, I heard voices and laughter. Rounding the corner, I saw small groups of people clustered at umbrella-shaded tables. I was briefly aware of women in shorts and striped shirts and sneakers; men in caps, boating shoes, chinos. I kept walking, hoping no one would notice the trespasser in their midst. And indeed my boater's disguise—jeans, T-shirt and Top-siders—must have been convincing because no one gave me so much as a passing glance.

Feeling more confident now, I strode down the hill toward the pier, where a couple of large cruising sailboats were tied up at the finger docks. On the foredeck of one of them a young man in cutoffs and bare feet was doing something with tape and a screwdriver; he was too absorbed in his task to even look up as I passed by. Further along, a gray-haired guy was cleaning his boat's topsides, hose in one hand, scrub brush in the other. He glanced my way, nodded hello, and went back to work.

I returned his nod and kept walking until I reached the

The pier and mooring field of the Nyack Boat Club. At this point, the Hudson River is almost three miles across, giving sailors lots of room to play. On the opposite (eastern) shore are the hills of Westchester County.

end of the dock. In the clear now, I stood admiring the view of sun-sparkling water, puffy white clouds and gleaming white boats. What a wonderful place!

I was savoring my illicit moments when I heard footsteps on the dock behind me. Uh-oh, I thought. This is it: eviction time.

"Great day," a deep voice said.

"Wonderful," I replied, turning.

The man was paunchy and red-haired and had the kind of tan that made you think he must live under his own hole in the ozone. But I needn't have worried about his intentions. Rather than booting me out, he had just come over to pass the time of day while he waited for his sailing buddies to show up for the afternoon races. He was friendly and chatty and before long he was even inviting me to come down and crew on race days.

"Ask anybody," he said. "People are always looking for crew."

Races? I hesitated. I knew nothing about race rules and procedures. But I remembered Diego's advice: "Race whenever you can. You'll learn twice as much and twice as fast as when you're just cruising around on your own."

I took the plunge. "Sure," I said. "When?"

Sundays were out. That was clear right up front. Sundays were for serious racers. Competition was cutthroat. Reputations were at stake. Trophies were won and lost. National rankings hung in the balance. It was no place for a beginner.

Wednesday evenings sounded like more my speed. The rules were not as rigorously enforced, the mood was informal, and everyone was more interested in having a good time than in setting records.

The next Wednesday evening I hurried home from work, changed into jeans and sneakers, packed a canvas bag with a windbreaker and a bottle of water, and dashed down to the

club. When I got there, skippers and crew were already assembling on the terrace. After asking around I found a skipper who was shorthanded and who didn't mind offering a
spot to a rank amateur.

Ron was a stocky, no-nonsense guy in his late-fifties.
Without fuss or formality he asked my name, introduced me
to the other member of his crew—his wife, Harriet—then
said, "Let's go," and led us down to the waterfront. Bing,
bing, bing. No jokes, no small talk. He was all business. I
wondered if this was going to be a good idea.

We boarded the club launch, which was filled to the gunwales with other racers: a chatty, enthusiastic bunch decked
out in peaked caps and bright-colored windbreakers.

Ron's boat turned out to be much like its owner: stocky
and no-nonsense. When I asked, he told me it was an Ensign,
but the name didn't mean anything to me. I later learned that
Ensigns were among the most popular day sailers ever built.
Twenty-two-and-a-half feet long, with full keels and big
roomy cockpits, they were heavy and reassuringly stable.
First built more than thirty years ago, they were enjoyed
both by white-knuckle racers and by families looking for
comfortable rides and easy handling.

As soon as we were aboard, Ron put Harriet and me to
work getting the cover off and the sails raised. Although he
continued brisk and businesslike, his sense of calm, solid
command soon put me at ease. When I later heard that he
was a retired New York City police detective, it made sense.
It was not hard to imagine him methodically bulldogging a
case: leaning on witnesses, probing for clues, pulling the ev-
idence together. But I was glad I did not know he was a cop
when we went out that evening. I would have been doubly
nervous about making mistakes.

My job was to man the jib sheets. Ron worked the tiller,
set our course, and decided on strategy, while Harriet handled the main sheet.

We'd be racing against a half-dozen other Ensigns, but as

we headed for the starting line, smaller, faster boats flew around us like madcap butterflies. Lasers, Thistles and Lightnings they were called, and you could tell the difference by their size and by the markings on their sails: red electrical bursts for the tiny 13-foot Lasers; purple-flowered thistles on the spunky 17-footers; blue lightning bolts for the swift 19-footers. They would start their races after we Ensigns got out of the way.

"Ever work a spinnaker?" Ron asked as he steered us toward the line.

"No. But I'm willing to learn. Just tell me what to do."

He did not seem perturbed. "No problem. We'll work it out."

"We haven't used the chute since last summer, so we're a little rusty ourselves," Harriet explained sympathetically. "Here." She handed me a pair of gloves that looked like golf gloves: leather-and-nylon panels with the fingertips cut off. "You'll need these," she said.

"I will?" It had never occurred to me that you'd need gloves for sailing.

"Trust me."

To anyone watching from shore it would have been hard to tell that our little fleet was in a race. In the faintest of breezes we crept over the starting line—an imaginary line running between a marker buoy and the committee boat. There was barely enough wind to keep us moving against the current. Some race, I thought. Still, Ron was determined to eke out every bit of advantage against our opponents as we crabbed upwind toward the first marker buoy.

It took us almost a quarter hour to get near the orange marker. "Prepare to come about," Ron said softly as we inched toward it. He kept his voice low so as not to alert our nearest competitor, a blue-hulled Ensign that was now creeping up on our starboard quarter.

"Ready about," whispered Harriet, her gloved hands on the main sheet.

"Ready about," I confirmed quietly. I had the starboard sheet wrapped around a winch and was set to release it the second Ron steered us into the wind and onto the opposite tack. Any delay, any sloppiness in getting the sail into position, would mean a loss of precious seconds in the turn.

Tension was high. Silently, like soldiers in the front line preparing to charge, Harriet and I waited for Ron's command.

The other boat was edging up on our starboard beam now, but we had the inside track on the turn, and if we did it right—came as close to the mark as possible without touching it (a penalty that would require us to go around again)—we'd grab the lead for the next leg.

Now the marker buoy was just off our bow. Another few seconds and it came amidships. Ron waited another beat or two, then gave the command: "Coming about," he said, and pushed the tiller to leeward. Slowly the bow started to turn into the wind. "Easy, easy," he warned me. "Don't let that sheet go too quickly."

The bow kept coming around through the breeze. The foresail started to collapse. "Now!" he said.

I released the starboard sheet just as the foresail collapsed. Then the wind caught it on the other side and pulled it around to port. Quickly I hauled on the portside sheet and got the jib set, all without costing us any of our momentum.

"Well done," said Ron, giving a thumb's up when we'd completed the turn and slipped ahead of the blue boat.

As we tacked along the next leg of the triangular course Harriet showed me how to get the spinnaker ready for the third leg, which was downwind. As soon as we made the turn around the next buoy the two of us got busy: hoisting the big candy-striped parachute sail; bracing it with a portable boom called a whisker pole, and then dropping the jib. It was a tricky business, what with lines getting crossed and the wind barely strong enough to keep the chute bellowed out in front of us. Then the next time we turned back upwind we had to quickly douse the chute and raise the jib again.

At every subtle shift of the wind or current Ron had us making minute adjustments to the sails: "ease up on the jib sheet;" "harden up the main;" "release the traveler;" "tighten up on the downhaul."

I was glad for the gloves. Harriet had been right: Without them my hands would have been shredded by the sheets whipping across my palms and through my fingers.

The big surprise was how exciting even a slow race could be. My adrenaline was pumping like mad as we fought to edge out other boats. And when we managed to beat our nearest rival to the finish line, even Ron's granite reserve cracked ever so slightly. "Good work," he said, offering a brief smile. We hadn't come in first overall, but we weren't dead last either.

As we headed back to the mooring in the fading light, I silently thanked Diego once again for his good advice. In one evening of racing I had learned more about sail management and tactics than I had learned in several seasons of random cruising.

Back at the clubhouse I joined Ron and Harriet for a beer on the terrace. Other racers stopped by to retell the race as they saw it, to embellish their own part in it, and to rag Ron for his.

"That's the great thing about sailing," said Al, the skipper of the winning boat. "It teaches you patience and humility."

"Unless you're racing," Ron replied.

"Then what?"

"It teaches you anger and arrogance."

It was all light-hearted and casual, and as I drove home afterwards I realized I might need to revise my preconceptions about the club. If Ron and Harriet and the others I had met were typical, the club might not be the bastion of old snoots that I had imagined.

I could have kept on that way, mooching rides and avoiding paying the fees to become a member of the club. But little by little I found my anarchist resistance being whittled away by the good will and friendliness of the people I met.

They were a diverse and quirky bunch and fit no particular profile. Whatever the criteria for membership might be, race, color, religion, gender or pedigree seemed to have nothing to do with it. A "workingman's club" was how I heard it described, and mostly that appeared to be true, though you'd have to add women to that description since women were some of the most active members and dedicated racers. The roster also included a fair number of upper-income professionals, to judge by the Mercedes and Acuras parked in the lot and the handful of oversized yachts out in the mooring field.

But most of the boats I crewed on were old and well-used cruisers in the 25-foot range, and most of the guys I sailed with earned their livings with their hands as well as their heads. One was an elevator engineer, another was a steelworker, another was a chiropractor. Riding the launch out to some skipper's boat, I might find myself talking with an insurance investigator or a volunteer fireman, a commercial airline pilot or a kindergarten teacher. I met social workers, a kosher butcher, a realtor, a welder, a park superintendent, a filmmaker, a nurse, a dentist.

The club was a co-op, a kind of do-it-yourself organization, which gave it an informal, down-home feeling. Instead of having a paid staff, it was run and maintained by the members themselves, each of whom was expected to show up a couple days a year to help out on one of the work crews. If a dock needed repairing or the clubhouse needed painting or the trees needed trimming, the members did the work themselves. One group launched the boats in spring and hauled them in the fall. Other crews laid out the moorings and maintained the club's launches and work boats. I liked that. It kept the dues down and was a good way to learn how to do stuff. It also meant avid, sweat-free social climbers would not be happy here. What brought people to *this* club was the love of boats and the water. The only status that seemed to matter was how willing you were to help out your buddies and, if you were a racer, how good you were.

I was hooked. By the end of that season I was ready to apply for membership.

What clinched my decision was the sale of my book. With my advance money in the bank, it was now only a matter of time before I'd have a boat of my own. And what better place to keep it than at the club, which was only five minutes from my house?

That fall, after recruiting a couple of sponsors from among the club's members, I sent in my application. Then I waited nervously for my interview. What kind of questions would they ask me? Would they want to test my nautical knowledge? My social skills?

I needn't have worried. The interview amounted to nothing more than a pleasant conversation with a couple of friendly people: an older man with close-cropped gray hair, and a woman I knew from crewing on her husband's boat.

The small clubroom where we met was comfortably decorated with brass lamps and nautical prints, and furnished with canvas-backed chairs and a round oak table. My interviewers gave me a little history of the club. (It was founded in 1902 and was originally a rowing club.) They outlined some of the rules and regulations, threw me a few powder-puff questions about my sailing experience, my profession and my family. And that was it. There were no bizarre rituals, no hazing, just friendly handshakes all around and a promise that I'd be notified shortly about the outcome. Sure enough, I received a letter a week or two later welcoming me as a probationary member.

At the club's next monthly meeting three other new members and I were asked to step forward. We were applauded, given keys to the building, and welcomed aboard by the commodore, the vice commodore, the rear commodore and various sub-commodoratti. I was in.

By the following spring, everything had fallen into place. I had found the boat I wanted and I now had a place to keep it: an assigned position in the club's mooring field. All I needed now was the mooring itself: the anchor to which I would tether Murdock's boat once I took possession.

Moorings come in a variety of shapes and sizes, ranging from small temporary anchors, or "lunch hooks," to heavy-duty permanent moorings designed to secure a boat over long periods and during heavy weather. The standard club mooring was the classic mushroom design: a heavy, cast-iron dish with an iron shaft rising from the center like the stem of an inverted mushroom. At the top of the shaft was an eye, to which the anchor chain was shackled.

Buying a new mushroom would have cost me a few hundred dollars. But some destiny must have been at work, because my first copy of the club's newsletter contained an ad for a three-hundred pounder that had been salvaged from the bottom of the river. The asking price: $100. Perfect. I phoned the seller immediately.

He was a hearty and voluble Irishman named Kieran and over the phone he told me more than I ever imagined there was to know about moorings: the merits of nylon versus Dacron lines, the appropriate length and size of chain for my size boat, the cost-versus-time ratio between buying ready-made mooring lines complete with eye-splices versus doing the splices myself. He even offered to teach me splicing. "It's easy," he said. "You can pick it up in fifteen minutes."

I demurred. I had too much to do right now to learn a new skill. But I agreed to pay Kieran what he was asking for his salvaged mushroom, which came to a lot less than a new one would have cost.

My next stop was Petersen's ships store, where Ed, the mooring specialist, helped me gather the necessary ground tackle: chains, shackles, swivels, nylon lines and stainless steel seizing wire. He also handed me a diagram showing how it all went together.

"I'd like a receipt," I said as Ed added up my purchases at the cash register. "I want to keep track of how much I'm spending."

Ed shook his head gravely. "That's not a good idea."

I laughed, thinking he was joking. But he was dead serious, and I understood why when I saw the bill. Thirty feet of chain, a half dozen shackles and swivels, fifty feet of nylon line—the costs were piling up.

I carried my carton full of chain and line out to my car, heaved it into the trunk, and drove down to the club.

On that early spring day the lower yard, where the boats were stored for the winter, was as busy as an anthill. The shriek of electric sanders, drills and saws filled the air as boat owners and their friends bustled about, preparing for the new season. Their boats were propped shoulder to shoulder on the metal or wood cradles where they had spent the winter. Blue plastic tarps—the boats' winter covers—lay in heaps on the gravel lot. Ghostly figures in white coveralls moved among the towering hulls. Their faces were covered with goggles and breathing masks and their coveralls were coated in the blue dust thrown off by sanded bottom paint.

Other owners, both men and women, scrambled under boats, paint brushes and rollers in hand, or climbed ladders with pails and cleaning brushes. The air was thick with acrid odors of paint, cleaners, thinners and the exhaust fumes from various small gas engines.

I found Kieran's mushroom lying where he said it would be: beneath his boat, along with the mushroom that he would keep for himself. I tagged mine with my name, then sat down on a bucket in the shade of Kieran's boat and got busy assembling my ground tackle.

Following the diagram from Petersen's, I started by attaching a large shackle to the eye at the top of the mooring shaft. To this shackle I attached the first length of chain, which ran to another shackle, which was attached to a swivel, then to another shackle, and so on, up to the pennants—the nylon lines whose spliced eyes would be looped over the cleats on the bow of the boat.

Time and again, in talking with Kieran, Ron and others, I had heard the same caution: The mooring system was only as strong as its weakest link. A corroded chain, a loose shackle pin, a pennant worn through by rubbing against the chocks—any of these could cost me my boat. With that scary thought in mind I double checked my shackle pins, tightened them with a wrench, secured them with wire. The possibilities for disaster seemed all too real.

Yet not everything was a worry. Sitting there amid the boats, I also found myself savoring the world around me. Amid the paint and solvent fumes and the gasoline exhaust I caught whiffs of the briny river. When there was a pause in the whine of power sanders I heard the throaty screech of gulls and the voices of men calling to each other, joking, asking for a hand.

Everywhere I felt the energy and excitement of sailors getting their boats ready, and it struck me that these sights and sounds and smells had been part of the rhythm of the waterfront since the days of Homer. The machinery was different and far noisier nowadays, but the routines were the same as they had been for countless generations of sailors as

ADVANCE tucked in for repairs at Petersen's boat yard in Nyack.

they prepared for fishing expeditions, battles or voyages of discovery. Hulls needed to be scraped and painted. Rigging needed upgrading. Rotted lines needed replacing, bright-work needed polishing, holes needed plugging. And here I was at last, in the middle of it all, and getting ready to embark on my own small moment in that great pageant. I loved it, and if anyone had noticed me there, they would have seen a quiet contentment on my face, interrupted only by the occasional wince of pain when a sharp end of stainless steel seizing wire pierced one of my fingers.

Once I had the mooring gear assembled and shackled securely to the mushroom, the next chore was to get the rig set in the mooring field. Kieran again came to my aid. Big, bearded and burly, he stood several inches over six feet tall and was built like a lumberjack. But as he soon demonstrated, it was mechanics not muscle that we needed to shift the heavy load of mushroom and chain.

Using a hand trolley—a kind of winch-on-wheels—we cranked the mooring and tackle up off the ground, then rolled the whole assembly over to the bulkhead. A motor-driven hoist stood at the water's edge and we used it to lower the mushroom onto a floating work platform that was known affectionately as "the cow." Firing up the cow's outboard, Kieran steered us out into the mooring field.

Laid out in March, after the threat of ice had passed, the mooring grid consisted of fifteen carefully spaced rows of plastic detergent bottles, with ten or twelve bottles in each row. Each bottle was marked with a letter (indicating the row) and a number (indicating position in the row), and each was held in position by a line tied to a cement block anchor that sat on the river bottom.

As a newcomer, I had been assigned a position out in Siberia: the row farthest from the shore, a good quarter mile out in the river. I preferred it that way, though. The fewer boats I had to sail around on the way to my mooring, the less likely I was to run into one of them. Besides, who knew what other mistakes I might make as I learned how this mooring business worked? I would much rather fumble around in private than provide entertainment for whoever might be watching from shore.

With Kieran steering and keeping an eye on the current, we arrived at the plastic bottle that marked my assigned position. The wind was cold out there. Despite a woolen sweater, woolen socks and long johns I was freezing and I was anxious to get the job done quickly.

But Kieran was a thorough teacher. Before I rolled the mushroom over the edge, he made sure I had the mooring chains laid out evenly on the deck, so they could play out evenly and not get snagged. He also warned me to keep clear of the chains. It was not hard to imagine the horrible consequences of a mistake: a foot caught in a coil, the chain pulled overboard as the three-hundred-pound weight plunged toward the bottom of the river, taking me down with it. I stepped back, as wary of that chain as of a coiled snake.

While Kieran positioned the cow beside the mooring marker, I checked one last time to make sure the float and pick-up stick were clipped securely to the loops on the upper ends of the pennants. I didn't want to dump the mushroom and chain over the side only to see the whole expensive package go straight to the bottom with no hope of retrieval.

Certain that everything was in order, I rolled the mushroom to the edge of the deck, then into the water. There was a satisfying splash, followed by the rattle of chain running out over the steel deck. At the same time, Kieran threw the outboard into reverse, which had the effect of taking up the slack on the pennants, which were still cleated to the deck. If things worked right, the anchor chain would be stretched out flat along the riverbed and the mushroom would be pulled over onto its side, allowing the edge of the dish to dig deep into the mud.

When we were sure we had a good set, I undid the mooring lines from the cleat and allowed the float and the pickup stick to be pulled overboard. The two floats bobbed nicely on the surface, just as they were supposed to do.

I grinned. Job done. Now I had a mooring. Now I was ready to bring my new boat up to its new home.

Before we were even off the cow, however, Kieran stepped on my expectations with both feet. "You want to wait a while to give the mushroom time to wedge its way down into the river bottom," he instructed as he steered us back to shore. "Let the mud wash over it for a week or so. Two to be on the safe side."

"Ah," I said reasonably. "Right. Good point."

Privately, though, I cursed and stamped. Wait? I didn't want to wait. I wanted to get the boat from Murdock now. Today. Right this minute. Damn caution. Damn Kieran's voice of experience. Damn, damn, damn.

# 7

# SAIL AWAY

*"Here's to the wind that blows, a ship that goes,*
*and the lass that loved a sailor."*
                                        —*Old sailors' toast*

I tried not to let the waiting get to me. I told myself that after all this time I could be patient a little while longer. But obsession had me by the throat. I found excuses to drive along River Road so I could gaze out at the boat, where it sat at Murdock's mooring. Walks with our gray terrier became opportunities to visit a hillside path, where I would stop to peer at the boat through my binoculars. At times I got so caught up in my reverie that the dog, having gone off on her own, would return to my side and sit looking up at me with her head tilted, as if she were wondering what was wrong with me.

I was goofy, in love, and reckless. Heading to work across the Tappan Zee Bridge, I'd hug the right-hand lane so I could catch a glimpse of my sweetheart as I went by. But this was not a good idea. The approach to the bridge included a long curving causeway, and if I kept my eyes on the boat for too long I might just miss the curve and go plunging straight through the guardrail and into the drink. This was more than infatuation. This was fatal attraction.

My waiting finally ended on a bright Sunday morning in April. The recommended two weeks had passed and I could now safely assume that the mushroom was thoroughly sunk in the mud and ready to take the weight of the boat. My dream was about to come true at last. On this day I would become skipper of my own boat.

To execute the transfer Murdock and I had agreed to meet on River Road, within sight of the spot where ECHO was moored. "I'll see you there at eleven hundred hours," I'd said, feeling giddily nautical.

I arrived early and stood gazing longingly at ECHO until Murdock turned up. We shook hands, I gave him my check, he gave me the title and registration, and the boat was mine.

"Congratulations," he said, and shook my hand again.

According to the old saw, the second happiest day of a man's life is when he buys his boat and the happiest day is when he sells it. But in our case the cliché was only half true. While I indeed felt elated, Murdock clearly took no pleasure in our transaction. Normally cheerful and talkative, he was subdued as he rowed us out to ECHO for what would be his last time aboard.

He took his time guiding me through the boat's details, making sure I knew where everything was and how everything worked. He started the outboard for me and let it warm up while he checked the radio, then looked around to see if he had missed anything. I was getting antsy, wanting to get moving while the tide was favorable. But still Murdock dawdled, as if reluctant to leave.

Pulling on my newly acquired sailing gloves (thank you, Harriet!), I told Murdock how much I appreciated all his help and reassured him that I could manage everything just fine now. Then I got busy hoisting the main and making ready the jib sheets and the furling line. Murdock took the hint. Shaking hands again, he let himself over the side and into the dinghy.

"I envy you," he said, as he untied the painter and began rowing away. "You'll have a great sail. They're calling for winds of . . ."

What was that? I wasn't really listening. It sounded like

he said "twenty to twenty-five." But that couldn't be right. It was a perfect, mild spring day. There was so little breeze on this patch of river that I would probably need the motor just to get out to where the wind was.

I gave Murdock a wave as he rowed away, then got down to business. I checked all the lines to make sure they were running free, with no knots or tangles. I listened to the motor to make sure it was running smoothly. Then I scrambled forward, pulled the pennants off the bow cleats, dropped them over the side along with the attached floats, and was free. No tether held me. My boat and I were on our own.

Scooting back to the cockpit, I threw the motor into gear, opened the throttle and steered for the middle of the river.

The wind was from the south, and there was barely enough of it to stiffen the main as I motored along. But once I got further out, beyond the protection of the hilly shore, the breeze picked up. I killed the engine, tugged on the port jib sheet to unfurl the genoa, and hauled in the sheets. The wind was my power now.

Glancing over my shoulder, I saw Murdock sitting on his oars watching me go. I grinned and gave him a wave, and he waved back, and I could almost feel the lines of affection that bound him to this boat stretching thinner and thinner as I sailed her away, until at some point they snapped and I could see him no longer.

On the chart, the straight-line distance between Murdock's mooring and mine added up to hardly more than a mile. But you couldn't get there in a straight line. The two-mile-long causeway that led up to the Tappan Zee Bridge stretched out from our side of the river like an enormous fence, separating the lower river from the upper. Low-slung motorboats could easily pass beneath it by slipping between the causeway's support columns. But bigger boats and those with masts had to make a long eastward detour and pass under the bridge itself, which at its highest point stood almost 140 feet above the shipping channel. That was where I headed now.

Sailing eastward parallel to the causeway, I aimed for the first big opening between the bridge supports, where I could slip through while still staying clear of the shipping lanes.

As I steered toward the east I could feel the south wind picking up strength. It was soon hitting the boat and the sails broadside, and hitting them so hard that the boat began to heel over. I was really clipping along now; the lee rail was almost in the water. How far over would this boat go, I wondered nervously as I leaned far back on the upwind side, my feet braced against the lee bulkhead. I thought about grabbing a life vest, but the nearest one was down below, in the cabin, and I didn't dare leave the tiller to get it—not with the boat tearing along this way. I wondered if I'd be able to reach the vest in time if the boat capsized.

But as I sailed along with my teeth gritted and my hand clamped tightly on the tiller, I remembered what Murdock had said—that more than once he had tried to tip the boat over in a high wind but had not been able to do it. At times he had forced the boat to lean so far over that she was sailing on her side and water was coming in over the gunwales. But she never went over all the way. All he had to do, he had told me, was to take his hand off the tiller. The boat would immediately turn her nose into the wind and pop upright. "That's how safe she is," Murdock had said.

Now, as I flew along, I began to see what he meant. Sitting high on the windward side, I used my weight as well as the tiller to balance the boat. The result was just what I had hoped for. Thanks to her heavy keel, the boat stayed right where I put her. I started to relax a little. Even to grin. Then to whoop with delight. What a great little boat she was!

By the time I reached the first big opening under the bridge and turned toward it, I wasn't worried about a thing. I was paying attention, I was alert, but I was not anxious or afraid. I had a feeling for the boat now. I knew I could handle her.

With the wind directly behind me now, I set the sails wing-and-wing: I had the mainsail swung all the way out to one side and the big foresail spread wide on the other, exactly like the wings of a bird. So beautifully was the boat balanced that I found I could stand with the tiller tucked between my knees and steer by simply leaning slightly to one side or the other.

And that was the way I slid under the bridge, standing, hands free, weight shifting this way and that on my feet as the boat and I danced upriver. From overhead came a steady roar of traffic: of trucks and busses and cars racing who knew where.

I thought of the many times I had driven over that bridge and admired the sight of sails on the river. How I had wished I were down on the water in a boat instead of hurrying over and away! Now here I was, just where I'd always wanted to be. With a satisfied grin, I imagined those motorists overhead looking down at me when I came clear of the bridge, looking down and envying my freedom, my beautiful boat with her wings spread wide.

As the wind held steady, carrying me effortlessly along, I let my eyes roam over the boat's curves and details: the white sails against the clouds; the soft glow of the teak trim on the cabin top; the steel-bright gleam of winches and cleats. I felt the sensual kiss of the wind on the back of my neck and drank in the briny smell of tidewater, the warmth of the sun. This boat, the river, this sunshine: they were mine, all mine. This must be what Buddhist meditation is like, I thought: full attention; full presence in the moment; full connection with the world around you. Full joy.

I was so thoroughly absorbed in what I was doing, and

having such fun, that I let the wind carry me far up river before the thought occurred to me that maybe I'd better head in. Almost three hours had passed since I'd left the house; Ellen would start worrying if I didn't turn up soon. Besides, I was getting hungry. I had not brought any food with me, and my one small bottle of water was now empty.

It was when I turned back toward the club that I got smacked—and smacked hard.

While the wind was behind me I had been unaware of just how much stronger it had become. Now, swinging the bow around and into the wind, I suddenly felt its full force. Not only was it blowing harder than before, it had also begun to veer around to the west and to fling vicious gusts in my direction. Suddenly my hat was gone, the boat was pitched over on its side, water was pouring in over the gunwales and soaking my shoes and everything was happening at once.

If anyone had come along with a camera just then, they could have caught a prizewinning picture of a new boat owner in the grip of absolute terror: mouth agape, eyeballs bulging, fist clenched on the tiller and every muscle straining. As the boat went tearing along, carrying me with it, I suddenly wondered if Murdock had ever had the boat this far over. Maybe she really could capsize.

But instinct and experience came to the rescue. Quickly I let out the main, spilling wind out at the same time I eased up on the tiller. With the pressure off, the sails were now loose and flapping wildly. But the boat was upright and the water was running out of the back of the cockpit through the drain holes as it was supposed to do.

"Okay, settle down," I told myself. "Take it easy. It's all right."

I took a deep breath, got the lines unscrambled and shifted position on the seat, which was now thoroughly soaked, as were my feet and trousers. Then, little by little I tightened up on the sheets and got sailing again. The gusts fell off, the wind steadied, and I turned the boat back toward the mooring field. The bow tossed glittering spray into the air, like a dog shaking itself dry after a bath.

By now the wind had shifted decisively around to the west and was again picking up strength. The sky was clouding over and the water ahead was turning ominously dark. I also noticed that there were no other boats on the river. Did everyone else know something I didn't? Never mind, I thought; I managed the last blow, I can manage this.

My foolish ignorance had given way to foolish over-confidence, and I did nothing to prepare for the blow I could plainly see was headed my way. I should have short-ened sail there and then, at least reefed in the genoa. In-stead, I sat there watching the line of dark water move toward me, and when the wind hit, it came in erratic gusts, shifting this way and that. Immediately I had another bat-tle on my hands, the boat leaning far over as it raced along, and me hanging on and wondering how long I could ride this thing.

I was flying down on the mooring field now, and with the waves getting higher and the wind blowing harder I could not think how I would be able to maneuver alongside the mooring stick and grab it.

Slowing down was the first order of business. For starters I eased out the main. Then I rolled up the genoa. Thank God for that roller-furling setup. Instead of having to climb out onto the pitching deck to lower the foresail by hand, all I had to do was grab the furling line and haul away, rolling the sail around the forestay. I was careful, though, to keep a little of the foresail open so I could maintain steering way, and that maneuver made a big difference. The boat slowed and straight-ened up, and from there on, despite the continuing wind, I was firmly in control.

Now all I had to do was get the boat moored and get my-self ashore. The problem was, the club launch wasn't running yet—it was still too early in the season. So I would have to bring my boat in to the club dock to collect a dinghy, then tow the dinghy out to the mooring so I could ferry myself back to shore once I had the boat tied up.

I was not about to come into the dock under sail, though. With the wind blowing as hard as it was, I was afraid I might damage my boat or someone else's. I'd have better control if I came in under motor power alone.

Turning into the wind so that it loosened its grip on the sails, I brought the boat almost to a standstill, then reached behind me and pulled the starter cord. Nothing happened. I pulled again. Still nothing. I adjusted the throttle, eased out the choke. No luck. The motor still wouldn't kick in. Shit! Without a motor there was no way I was going to approach the dock in these conditions. So how was I going to get ashore?

My only recourse was to head for my mooring and hope that someone would come along in a dinghy to pick me up.

With catching a mooring, as with so much else in life, timing is everything. The trick is to approach from downwind and bring the boat to a stop just as the bow comes level with the pickup stick. Then you scramble forward, grab the stick, and haul it and the mooring lines aboard.

I managed the first parts okay. Turning into the wind and letting go of the sheets, I brought the bow up alongside the stick. Then, letting go of the tiller, I climbed over the cabin top and out onto the pitching foredeck. But my timing was off. By the time I grabbed for the stick the boat had been carried backwards by the current and the stick was out of reach. Glancing around, I saw I was drifting toward another boat.

Quick, back to the cockpit. Tighten up the main. God, I'm too close to that other boat. I'm going to hit it. Got to swing away, get the bow turned. I pull hard on the tiller. Come on, turn, turn. . . .

Finally the bow comes around and we slide past the other boat, missing it by inches. As soon as I am clear of it, I circle around and nose up to my mooring once more. Crouching, one leg cocked beneath me, ready to spring, I aim for the stick, trying to bring the bow right alongside without running over it. Easy, easy. Here comes the stick. Now! I drop the tiller, let go the sheet and leap for the foredeck. I reach for the stick. This time it rolls into my hand, neat as you please.

Quickly I pull the tall-buoy aboard, haul in the mooring lines, and snug them tight over the bow cleats. With that the boat stops and stays put, reined in like a runaway horse.

I sit back on my heels and take a deep breath. I have done it. My boat and I are home. Or rather, the boat is home. I am still a quarter mile out in the river, amid whistling wind and white-capped waves. And I still have no idea how I am going to get ashore. All I can do is hope that someone will come by and give me a lift.

First, though, I have things to do. Crawling back to the mast on my hands and knees, I lower the flapping mainsail, secure it beneath its canvas cover, secure the halyard and the sheets, close the cabin.

All the while I keep a lookout for a ride back to shore. Spotting one of the club's tin boats in the distance, I shout, wave my arm over my head. But the wind is too strong. The driver doesn't hear me and doesn't look my way. Finally I do the sensible thing. Opening the cabin again, I get out the air horn that Murdock thoughtfully included with the boat's safety gear. I give it a blast that nearly shatters my right eardrum. But it does the trick. The boat changes course and heads in my direction.

He's coming at me so fast that I'm afraid he won't be able to stop in time and will ram into me. But at the last second the driver, who wears a yellow slicker and a peaked cap, expertly swings the bow away, throttles down, and stops precisely alongside.

"Boy, am I glad to see you," I tell my rescuer as I step down into the tin boat and take a seat amidships. "I wasn't looking forward to spending the night out here."

"Been known to happen," he says matter of factly, as though such a possibility were no big deal. Then he revs the outboard and we go roaring toward shore.

I turn and give ECHO one last look. Tugging at her mooring lines, she prances in the waves like a thoroughbred who's just raring to go again. Not me. I need a breather.

# 8

# SHAKE DOWN

*"Avast belay, yo ho, heave to,*
*A'pirating we go."*

—Peter Pan, *J.M. Barrie*

I was spooked and didn't mind admitting it. Even after a good stiff drink, I wasn't sure when or whether I'd ever be raring to go again. As much as I'd loved the early part of my trip upriver—all that glorious sunshine, that steady breeze, my own boat under my feet—in the end I'd been scared witless by the rising wind and chaotic waves. And it didn't help that the motor had let me down at a crucial moment.

If I'd had a coach, it would have been a good time for a pep talk: "Don't be a wuzz," he'd have said. "Are you going to let one rough ride stop you? What are you going to do now, get rid of the boat? Pack up your dreams?"

Well, no, I wasn't about to quit. Sure, my thoroughbred had given me a wild ride. But she didn't throw me off, did she? In fact I had handled her really well even when the wind was at its worst. *And* I'd brought her home under sail alone! That was nothing to be ashamed of. I just needed more experience.

Still, I would have felt a lot better if I knew I could rely on the outboard. Had I done something wrong when I tried to start the little Merc? I remembered that Murdock had coaxed it to life with the very first pull of the cord. Had I missed a step? Did I pull the cord the wrong way? Somehow or other I'd need to figure out the problem and fix it if I was going to feel safe going out on the river.

My next attempts were not encouraging. Sometimes it

would kick in, sometimes not. Sometimes it would run smoothly for a few minutes, then cough and die. I tried pulling the cord once, waiting a few minutes, then pulling again. I tried starting it with the choke open, then with it closed. I checked the fuel line for leaks but found nothing wrong. Ditto the fuel filter. I began to think that Mr. Cranky had a mind of his own. Either that or the river gods had decided that I had not been punished enough for my presumption on that first outing, when I had dared to claim the wind and sunlight and water were mine, all mine. Looking back at my journal entries, I can find no other explanation for Mr. Cranky's erratic behavior:

May 5th, Sunday:
A great morning for sailing. Looking toward the river from the top of our street, I could see the sun flickering off the water. There were waves out there, a breeze for sure. Perfect.

I gulped down bagel and coffee, grabbed sunscreen, cap, water and ditty bag, and gave Ellen a kiss. "Back at noon," I said, and hurried out the door.

I didn't have much time. There were errands to run in the afternoon, places to be. And it was already after nine when I parked near the club. Rushing down to the dock, I hopped into a tin boat, cranked the engine, and barreled out to ECHO at full throttle. I was eager to use every minute of sailing time.

Pulling alongside ECHO, I scrambled aboard. I tied the tin boat's painter to a cleat on the transom and hurried through my preparations: stowed my gear, loosened the sheets, got the cover off the main. Then, turning my attention to the outboard, I took a hopeful breath and pulled the starter cord.

Brrrrup! The little Merc kicked in on the first pull. I waited nervously, wondering if it was going to keep going. It did, bless its metallic little heart.

With that worry settled, I hurried forward and cast off the mooring lines. Then I scrambled back to the cockpit, threw the motor into gear and got underway, heading back to the dock to drop off the tin boat so the next guy could use it. As I neared the dock, though, I realized that in my hurry I had neglected to set my dock lines and fenders.

There I was, in the middle of the mooring field, surrounded by a whole armada of expensive boats, with a strong current trying to push me sideways upstream, where I stood a good chance of hitting at least one of them and maybe more.

I had a choice: either play it safe and get clear of the mooring field before setting the lines, or risk doing the job on the spot. But playing it safe would take too much time. I looked around. The nearest boat was still a good distance away. If I was quick about it I might just beat the current . . .

I threw the motor into neutral and left the tiller, allowing the boat to drift. Dashing below, I grabbed a couple of lines from where they lay coiled on the banquette. Then I hurried back up to the cockpit. I checked my drift. The distance between me and the next boat had shrunk. But I was still okay. Quickly I looped one line around a stern cleat, then hurried forward to secure a line to the bow. I'd skip the fenders. Rigging them would take too much time. Anyway, the dock was somewhat cushioned, so if I was careful I might not get too banged up.

Putting the motor into gear once more, I turned ECHO's nose into the current and eased her toward the touch-and-go dock at the end of the pier. She was barely moving as I brought her alongside. My angle and speed were right. She kissed the dock without so much as a bump or a scrape. Quickly I stepped off, dock lines in hand, and got her tied down at the bow and stern.

I left her there with the motor idling while I untied the tin boat and motored it over to its home dock. Then I jogged back to ECHO, cast off the lines, gave the boat a shove, climbed aboard and steered for the fairway—the wide path that ran down the middle of the mooring field.

That's when I got another lesson thrown in my face.

I was in the middle of fairway, heading happily toward open water, when the motor gurgled, sputtered and died. Now what? I felt a stab of panic.

I tried to restart the motor. Once, twice, three times. No luck. I was adrift, the current was running strong, and unless I thought of something fast I was going to be pushed into the bowsprit of that magnificent 35-footer that was moored maybe a hundred feet off my port bow. To make matters worse the wind was starting to pick up, adding to the drift.

What to do? I hadn't thought to set the mainsail before leaving the dock; without it I had no backup power to draw on. I could throw out the anchor and stop the drift, but the anchor was down below, in the forward compartment and there was no time to get it out. The gap between that bowsprit and me was getting smaller by the second and unless I did something fast I was going to crash into it in about half a minute.

That's when I suddenly realized I had one option left: the genoa, my other power source.

In a rush I loosened the sheets and the furling line, let the big foresail run out, then quickly sheeted it in. Instantly it caught the wind and I had power again. I let the jenny pull the bow around. It swung clear of the other boat just in time, barely missing that pricey bowsprit.

Shaken by the close call, I threaded my way through the other moored boats and headed for open water. My pulse was still racing and it took a while for it to settle down. I hated to think what could have happened if I hadn't moved as quickly as I did. My boat and the other guy's could have been wrecked, and all because I had been in too much of a hurry to do the job right from the start.

The hell of it was, my shortcuts probably cost me more time than they'd saved, what with trying to correct for the mistakes I'd made. As for the fear-driven spike in my blood pressure, who knew what that had cost me? Fifteen minutes off the end of my life? An hour?

Free of the mooring field at last, I sat back and savored a quiet hour of coasting and tacking in fair winds. The sky was a brilliant blue, the river danced with light, the waves tossed merrily off the bow. It was a splendid interlude and I was grateful for every moment.

Too soon, though, I had to turn back. My time was running out and I was determined to get home by noon as promised. I knew Ellen worried about me being out in the boat alone. I didn't want to make it worse for her by keeping her guessing.

Luckily Mr. Cranky decided to cooperate on the way back. Whatever had caused his indigestion in the middle of the fairway, he now seemed in fine health and willing to give me the push I needed to get back to the club. This time, too, I remembered to set the fenders, so docking was not as worrisome as it had been on the way out. Then came the rest of the job: pick up a tin boat again, tow it out to the mooring, catch the tall buoy, haul the mooring lines aboard and tie everything down securely before ferrying myself to shore.

I got back to the car just before noon. That was the good news. The bad news was, I felt tired and discouraged. I couldn't help but wonder what I had gotten myself into by becoming a boat owner. Was it always going to be like this: a lot of effort for very little payoff? Never mind that much of life fits that same description. Sailing is supposed to be different: a refuge, not another burden. I only hope that the process will get easier the more I do it.

And yet the morning was not a complete washout. Far from it. I enjoyed a wonderful hour of sailing, and came away with some valuable lessons. From now on I will make sure that everything is in working order and ready to go *before* I leave the mooring: fenders out, dock lines at hand, mainsail up in case the motor quits. And in case the wind drops as well, I'll keep the anchor in its locker under the foredeck, where it's within easy reach; then if all else fails I'll at least have a chance to keep the boat from drifting into trouble.

I won't rush my departures, either. If I don't have time to do the preparations right, I won't go out at all.

By the middle of summer I was sailing regularly: once, sometimes twice a week. As I had hoped, getting started did indeed get easier and quicker with each outing. I also made sure the boat and I were well prepared before I cast off.

The dybbuk inside the motor, however, continued to play his wicked games with me. I never knew when he was going to cooperate. Every cruise became an exercise in anxiety: would the motor start or wouldn't it? And if it started, would it keep going?

I didn't have a clue what to do about the problem. I was too intimidated by the thing to even risk taking the cover off the housing to look inside. Besides, what would be the point? I wouldn't know what I was looking at.

Finally, frustrated after yet another motor failure, I telephoned Murdock. After all, he was the one who had saddled me with this evil contraption.

On the phone Murdock seemed unconcerned. "It sounds like you're flooding it," he told me. "I'll come over and take a look."

We met at the dock, where we climbed into a tin boat and motored out to ECHO. Once aboard, Murdock unhooked the fuel line, then confidently undid a clip at the back of the motor and removed the cover. Using a wrench from my tool kit, he unscrewed the spark plugs and wiped off the oily gunk that coated their sparking ends. Then, before reinserting the plugs, he pulled the engine's starter cord a few times, blowing the excess gas out of the cylinders. A fine mist of gasoline made rainbow puddles on the water. I thought of the EXXON VALDEZ and hoped there weren't any fish or lawyers nearby.

"You could try squirting a little injector fluid in there, too," he advised as he screwed the plugs back in.

"Ah," I said, and jotted a note. "Where do I get that?"

"Any auto parts store will have it. Okay, let's try again."

He put the cover back on, reattached the fuel line and pulled the cord. Barooom! A cloud of blue smoke erupted as the outboard kicked in. It kept purring nicely, too. Problem solved. Easy as pie—at least when Murdock did it. But would it work for me?

It did, as I discovered the next time the motor crapped out. Boldly removing the cover, I tried Murdock's plug-cleaning routine. The fix worked fine, but only for a short time. I tried new plugs and bought a can of fuel injector, which I squirted into the cylinder. Bingo! Success! But it crapped out on me again the next time.

This was maddening. True, my mechanical skills were improving. I was no longer afraid of taking off the cover and pulling the plugs. But I was no nearer to identifying the problem. My only consolation was learning that the dilemma was not mine alone.

"Of course you can't get your motor started," I was told by one boat clubber when he heard me grousing. "You're the owner."

He may have thought he was joking, but his illogical explanation seemed to reflect the bitter truth all too accurately.

One afternoon, as I proudly welcomed my friend Howard aboard ECHO for the first time, I prepared the lines and the sails, then prepared to start the motor. I approached it with a queasy mixture of hope and dread. Would it make a monkey out of me yet again? I lowered the prop into the water, checked to make sure there was gas in the tank, hooked up the gas line, squeezed the priming bulb, shifted the clutch into neutral and pulled the starter cord. Nothing. I pulled again. And again. Still nothing happened. Sweat was now dripping off my eyebrows.

"Here, let me have a try," said Howard.

"Be my guest," I said, but I was skeptical. Why should he have any better luck than I did? But damn if the thing didn't kick in for him after one pull on the cord.

I was dumbfounded. "How did you do that?"

Howard shrugged. "I just pulled. It seems to work fine."

"Great," I said, though I remained baffled. Sure enough, the next time I went out, the motor balked once more. Was I not pulling hard enough? Was I pulling too hard? I felt like kicking the thing. But I held back. Some little voice was telling me that I'd get better results if I spoke in soothing and respectful tones. Otherwise I might risk offending whatever demon had taken up residence inside.

It dawned on me then: somewhere I had crossed a line. I had acquired the sailor's disease. I had become superstitious.

Sailors knew better than to whistle when they were at sea; they risked whistling up a storm. They did not speak ill of their ships or mention anything about priests or parsons while on board: "No black coats, mister," warned one old sailor, "not if you want to see land."

I saw now that such magical thinking was a reasonable response to the unfathomable mysteries of the sea, and that the same applied to outboards. Mine clearly had a mind of its own, and I was convinced that I must treat it well and say only good things about it. In return, maybe the cold-hearted little bastard would repay my kindness by behaving itself.

My strategy seemed to work, too. Although I still dreaded every encounter with Mr. Cranky, by the middle of that first summer I had developed what appeared to be an effective routine. Taking the starter cord in hand, I would give it a mighty pull. Invariably my first effort ended in failure. But did I rant and curse? Did I pound the motor with my fist? I did not. Staying calm, I would let my friend sit quietly for a while, giving him time to decide whether or not to co-operate.

While I waited, I would undo the sail cover and make sure all the lines were ready at hand and running free. I'd arrange my water bottle and snacks so that I could put my hands on them easily once I was underway. I'd get out a life jacket and hang it in a handy place, just inside the cabin door. And one morning in July I even took the opportunity to do something really risky. I changed the boat's name.

I knew I was on treacherous ground. Changing a boat's name was said to be bad luck, an invitation to disaster. But I was still new enough to sailing that I believed I could

The view from the cockpit of ADVANCE: sails in trim, the waters calm and a whole world of adventure beckoning just over the horizon.

pick and choose among superstitions, ignoring the ones I found to be inconvenient. A day of reckoning would probably come and I would regret my skepticism. For now, though, my need to put my personal stamp on the boat overrode any such anxieties. I crossed my fingers and went ahead.

Reaching for my brand new life ring, I hung it from its mount on the stern rail, where it proudly showed the world the boat's new name, displayed in plastic stick-on letters: ADVANCE.

The name was Ellen's idea and it fit perfectly, signifying both forward motion and the way the boat was bought and paid for: with the up-front money from my publisher. (Only much later did I discover the happy coincidence that ADVANCE was the name of the world's first centerboard boat: that innovative packet sloop built in Nyack in 1815.)

Granted, the name on the life ring was a half-way measure. In the fall, when the boat was out of the water, I would finish the job by sanding the old name off the transom and painting the new one there, making it permanent and official. But for now the life ring would do nicely to proclaim my boat's new identity and new spirit.

With the life ring in position on the stern rail, I turned my attention once more to my temperamental friend. Hoping that the motor had had enough time to sulk, I leaned over the transom and gave it a friendly pat on its cover. "Good boy," I said, and pulled the starter rope. As if to reward my affection, the motor sputtered, choked, then roared to life. I sat watching it warily for a minute, wondering if it would keep going. When it did I felt like cheering. But I restrained myself. No point in tempting fate, right?

Motoring clear of the mooring field, I let the engine run for a while longer, thinking it might appreciate the exercise. Then I hit the off button, set the sails and let the wind take over. Content now, I settled back, tiller in hand, and headed upriver, against the current. That way, if the motor failed me on the way back and the wind died as well, the current could carry me back down to the mooring.

I was in no hurry. I had a long weekend off from the office, and although Ellen and I planned to be away for most of that time, today was my day for the boat. With the whole day ahead of me, I looked forward to stretching my sailing limits. My usual cruising grounds extended no more than two or three miles from the club. But today I would aim further and give myself something interesting to look at as well. I would head for Sing Sing, the sprawling prison complex that rose up the hillside on the river's eastern shore, four or five miles to the north and east.

From our side of the river the place did not look at all like the terrifying lockup depicted in the Cagney movies: the Big House where New York's toughest criminals went when they were sent "up the river." True, at night the vast complex shone as an ominous island of light across the dark water, a floodlit city where darkness was to be feared. By day, though, the distant lockup looked more like a pretty little walled village or another rich man's fantasy estate. Red brick walls reminiscent of an English garden rose up the hillside and enclosed a large grassy area. Even through binoculars the place didn't look particularly ominous.

With the fresh breeze out of the west, I was carried north on a comfortable beam reach. I was bucking a strong southbound current, so it took almost an hour and a half for me to reach the red channel marker that was my target. Sure enough, I had a fine view of the prison: the fortress-like walls of red brick and gray stone, the guard towers set into the walls every few hundred yards. Overlooking the big grassy area in the middle of the complex, where tiny figures moved—playing soccer? jogging?—were the massive walls of the cellblocks. Slit windows faced the river like gun ports.

Amid these beautiful green hills, on the shores of this sparkling blue river, with a crystal sky and puffy white clouds overhead, it was hard to imagine how awful life must be for the men living behind those walls. But maybe that was the worst punishment of all. Other prisons that I had seen were set in bleak and barren landscapes: in the deserts of Arizona, on the empty plains of the Dakotas, or in the midst of New Jersey's industrial wastelands. But Sing Sing overlooked one of America's most spectacular landscapes, and it was hard to tell which might be worse: to spend years looking out at empty desert or to be cruelly subjected to this stunning vista of river and hills and sky: so close, so open and free and yet so utterly out of reach.

As I rounded the red buoy and turned back toward home, I couldn't help wondering how many eyes were watching my sails from behind those slit windows, and whether the sight was a gift or a curse: an encouraging vision of freedom or a maddening reminder of the impossibility of escape.

The westerly breeze that had carried me upriver now blew fair to carry me home on one long straight run, without any need for tacking. But the wind dropped abruptly when I came level with Hook Mountain, a high, rock-faced lump that rises over seven hundred feet above the western shore and effectively walls off that part of the river from any winds coming out of the west. In the mountain's shadow, I found myself drifting. The sails flapped lazily and if the Merc hadn't agreed to cooperate, I would have lolled around for hours while the current slowly carried me down the river. But with my first pull of the starter cord my friend growled happily to life and pushed me back down to my mooring. Despite myself I was beginning to believe that gentle words and tender consideration might be having a positive effect on the little bast . . . , my little buddy. Superstitious? Me? I'd deny it to anyone. But I'd keep my fingers crossed just in case.

Back at the mooring, I took extra care in securing the boat. While Ellen and I were away on a weekend trip a hurricane would be working its way up the coast. If it came up the Hudson Valley ADVANCE would be right in its path. I checked her mooring lines and was reassured. They still looked as good as new and were well protected with chaffing gear at the places where they fed through the chocks to the cleat on deck. I furled the sails tight and wrapped extra lines around them. Then I cleared the decks of anything superfluous that might catch the wind. The mooring ball and pickup stick, which I usually kept tied down on the foredeck, now went below into the cabin. I checked the halyards and sheets to make sure they were snug. Then I locked her up. As I motored away in the tin boat I couldn't help wondering if AD-VANCE would still be there when I got back on Monday.

That weekend, whenever I had a chance, I checked in with the weather channel. My anxiety grew by the hour as I watched the storm track up the East Coast. Sure enough, it was headed right for New York City. Was this what my life was going to be like from now on? Was I doomed to be forever fretting about my boat's safety?

Ruefully I recalled an epigram I had once read: "The more money, the more worries; the more fat, the more worms." The writer was a long-ago rabbinic sage, but I was willing to bet he was also a boat owner.

In the end, the hurricane only sideswiped New York. Still, as we drove home that Sunday afternoon the radio was reporting extensive damage along the coast and up the Hudson Valley. Trees were down, power was out in many places, and the storm surge had battered the coast.

The minute we came through the door I checked the answering machine. One of the messages was from the chair of the club's mooring committee. The news was not good:

"Tom, if your boat is at mooring Oh-Twelve, I'm afraid it's been dismasted."

I felt my stomach sink. Oh, my beautiful boat. I groaned as I listened to the rest of the message:

"We pulled the mast aboard and got it tied down okay.

But the damage is pretty bad. If that's you—it looks like a sixteen- or seventeen-foot sloop—you'll want to tend to it as soon as possible."

Deeply shaken, I grabbed my gear, ran out to the car, and rushed down to the club. Dark clouds raced low across the sky. The wind was still high, churning the river to a brown froth. I could hear thunder growling off to the south, the back end of the hurricane. I pulled on a life jacket, jumped into a tin boat, cranked the motor, and headed out into the tumult of waves and wind.

I knew it was stupid of me to be out there. Chances were I wouldn't be able to do anything about the boat once I got to it. But I had to see it for myself, just to be sure. Because the more I thought about that phone message, the more I doubted that it was my boat he was talking about. Although he had given me the right position number, what he described was a smaller boat than ADVANCE. Either he had the mooring number wrong or he had the boat wrong, and I wouldn't breathe easy until I found out which.

Far out in the river now, at the farthest end of the mooring field, with the waves tossing me around like a cork in a washing machine, I was finally able to get a good look at ADVANCE. What I saw lifted my spirits even higher than the whitecaps that were throwing themselves against the tin boat's bow. Although she was bucking and tossing at her mooring lines, ADVANCE was as shipshape as she had been on the day I had left her: lines secure, sails snug beneath their covers, mast and shrouds perfectly intact.

Relief swept over me. The phone message had been a mistake. All I had to do was glance around me to see where the real damage had been done. The boat next to mine, a small day sailer, looked as if it had been attacked by an axe murderer. There was a gash down one side of her cabin top and a dent in her bow. Her rigging lines were strewn across her decks. Her broken mast lay lengthwise along her deck, where it had been secured by whoever had come to her rescue.

As I circled the wreck, I tried to imagine what had caused her mast to come down. A worn shroud? A loose or broken turnbuckle? Surely there was a lesson here, and I resolved to check my standing rigging as soon as I could. For now I would try to track down my neighbor and let him know what had happened to his boat. Whoever he was, he faced a lot of work and a lot of repair bills before he could sail again.

As I headed back to shore, I breathed a prayer of gratitude to the gods of wind and sea for having spared ADVANCE. I kept my voice to a whisper, though. Who knew what the deities might have in store for the future?

July 20th, Thursday:

I skipped out of the office early this afternoon to work on the boat. The day was too perfect to stay glued to my desk.

After changing into jeans and a T-shirt, I brought the boat into the dock and got to work with a scrub brush, a hose and a bottle of cleaning detergent. River scum had left my nice white hull stained yellowish brown around the water line. And down below it was crusted with barnacles. Some racers in the club haul their boats every few weeks to wax the hulls and clean the bottoms. I'm not that fanatical, but I am proud enough to want my baby looking her best.

I spent a couple of hours scrubbing the hull. Stretched full length on the dock, I reached under the boat as far as I could with a plastic ice scraper and chiseled off the barnacles. By the time I was done the hull gleamed and I was sweaty, tired and hungry.

"Have fun?" Ellen asked when I got home.

Fun? That wasn't exactly how I'd have described it, but I managed to sound enthusiastic. "Yeah, it was great," I said, then headed for the shower.

The truth is, the boat can be a drag sometimes. Often I seem to spend less time sailing than I do fixing and cleaning and cursing because things don't work. I am not the only one who feels this way. All I have to do is spend an hour at the club and I'm sure to hear some guy kvetching about the work and worry that his boat is inflicting on him. It happened just the other day, as a bunch of us stood on the dock waiting for the launch to take us out to our boats.

One of the guys—Gary, I think was his name—nodded toward the mooring field and said, "I looked out there after I got back from vacation, and damn it, the boat was still there. I'd been hoping somebody would steal it."

The rest of us laughed, but clearly he was only half joking.

Obviously all boat owners share this dilemma. But I am learning that it is not a good idea to grumble too much at home about all the problems that our boats inflict on us. Spouses and children will want to know, quite reasonably, why we don't just get rid of the damn things. But does a golfer give up the game because he's made a few lousy shots? Does a trout fisherman throw away his hip boots after a bad day of fishing? Of course not, for there is more to such pursuits than sweet reason can abide.

July 22nd, Saturday:
I almost did not go out on the boat this past weekend. Since I would be tied up with social obligations on Sunday, I knew I'd have to go out on Saturday or not at all. But when the launch dropped me off at the boat, I began to have second thoughts. The wind was stiff, gusting from the northwest, and whitecaps were stampeding toward me like a herd of wild horses, white manes flying. Overhead the racing clouds were dark and menacing. According to the forecast, though, the really strong winds would not hit until the afternoon. I could probably squeeze in an hour or so of sailing before the worst of it hit. Besides, this was my one chance all weekend. It was now or never.

My mind made up, I hoisted the main, then scrambled forward to the bow. Beneath me the boat was bouncing madly on the surf. Nervously I double-checked the ties on my life vest, though what good the vest would do me I could not imagine. If I went overboard out here, who would know? I could drift downstream for hours without anyone finding me. But I tightened my grip on the bow rail and pushed the fear aside. If I moved carefully and paid attention I had nothing to worry about.

I unwrapped the lines of the mooring ball and the tall buoy, secured them to the pennants, then worked the pennants off the chocks and let them go, setting the boat adrift. Quickly now, keeping one hand on the boat and watching my footing, I worked my way back to the cockpit and took hold of the tiller. I sheeted in the main, turned the bow away and let the wind take me. I didn't even try to start the motor. Who needed a motor with a wind like this?

As soon as the mainsail filled, the boat gathered speed and was soon flying out of the mooring field. It was like sledding down a steep hill. I hung on tight and let out a sound that was somewhere between howl of terror and a shriek of delight. Wow, what a ride! I tacked, jibed, dashed across the waves this way and that. I was following no course, just zipping around as the mood took me. I was having a ball. My only companions on the river were the gulls overhead, who seemed to be having as much fun as I was, swooping and wheeling as if for no other reason than to savor the pleasure of riding the wind.

But I could feel the wind getting stronger, too, making the boat harder to handle. I had the genoa reefed down to the size of a dishtowel, but I still had too much sail exposed. The boat was leaning far over. Water was whooshing over the lee gunwales and I had to fight to keep the back corner of the main from dragging in the water, where it could pull the boat right over. Nor could I shorten the main because I hadn't yet figured out how to do that. I could experiment, but this was not the time or the place. At the moment I had my hands full just keeping the boat upright.

Hoisting the mainsail, I prepare for an evening cruise. *Photo by Gwen Samuels*

I kept at it for almost half an hour. The battle was exhilarating, but exhausting, too, and with the wind rising I finally conceded that it was the time to retreat, both for my own good and also for the sake of any poor fool ashore who might be tempted to follow my example and come out and play. I hated to think I might be responsible for someone else's disaster.

The only problem now was getting back in. Not having hooked up the gas line or primed the motor, and with no hope of doing either in this tumult, I'd have to get in under sail—a tricky maneuver. I turned downwind and flew back toward mooring field, wind whistling in the rigging, my hat blowing off (reminder: buy hat clip), my glasses threatening to blow off (reminder: replace frayed Croaker with a new one).

In minutes I was coming up on my mooring. At least, I thought it was my mooring. But something didn't look right. I could see my float ball. But where was the pick-up stick? Did it sink? Did I forget to secure it to the ball when I left? Dumb, dumb, dumb. Damn thing was brand new, too. Twenty-five bucks down the toilet.

But there was no time to lament the loss. The float ball was coming up fast. But how in the hell would I grab it without a pick-up stick? Ah! The boat hook! That's what I needed. But I had to think: Where did I stow the hook? In the cabin? In the locker under the seat? And how would I scramble around looking for it and still manage the boat? Because suddenly I was there: at the edge of the mooring field, boats lined up to north and south of me and I had to find my way past them and over to my mooring without hitting anything. This was going to be tough.

I told myself to calm down and get away from the other boats so I had some elbowroom. I threw the tiller over, spun the boat away and went careering back toward open water.

When I was well clear of the other boats, I headed downwind on a broad reach, steadying the boat so I was free for a few seconds to go hunting for the hook. If it were down below, in the cabin, I'd be in trouble. I'd have to leave the tiller to go look for it, which would be really hairy in these conditions. But I got lucky. Lifting the seat cover, I peered into the lazarette and saw the pole down at the bottom. I leaned into the deep locker, reached for the pole, and grabbed it just as the seat lid slammed down on my back. (Reminder: find a way to latch that cover open.) Still, I had the pole now. I pulled it and myself back up into the cockpit and paused to catch my breath.

I looked around to get my bearings, and . . . Wait! What was that over there? Could it be? Dead ahead, about 500 yards and just barely visible over the whitecaps, was my missing tall buoy. It was bobbing merrily along by itself, heading downriver as if enjoying its freedom to roam. Somehow, in my anxiety about casting off, I must have forgotten to clip it securely to the pennants. Off it went, carried away by wind and current. It was a mere fluke that I happened to stumble upon it again. And there I was, heading right for it.

Holding my course, I slid neatly alongside, grabbed the stick, and hauled it aboard. Man, was I lucky or what!

But I was not done yet. I still had to get back to the mooring and grab the float. Turning, I headed into the north wind, set up my approach to the float, and got the hook ready.

To allow for the current, I aimed to stall the boat just a little upstream from the float, then drift back to where I could reach beneath the float with the boat hook and grab the line that tethered it to the pennants. But I let out the mainsail too soon, stalling the boat too far downstream for me to reach the float. Worse, I was now drifting back toward a neighboring boat.

Quickly I sheeted in the main, caught the wind and used its power to carry me clear. Then, turning back, I came around a second time. But again I miscalculated, stalling too soon in the stiff wind, which again left me too far from the ball. I had no choice. I needed to go around a third time.

By now I was beginning to think I should just give it up. Go for one of the guest moorings, which at least had a pick-up stick I could grab. But that would only delay a solution. I'd still have to get the boat back to my own mooring at some point, and who knows when I'd have time for that? No, it was better to get the job done now.

Swinging out into open water again, I came around once more. This time I got it right: came up on the float, slid the bow alongside it before stalling, then scurried up to the bow before the current had a chance to carry the boat away again. Reaching over the side with the hook, I snagged the tether on the first try, just as the current was starting to carry the boat out of reach. Quickly I hauled in the float and pennants, then looped the pennants over the cleats on the fore-deck and made them secure. Whew. At last! I was home.

Kneeling there, my face in the rising wind, I took a deep breath of relief and satisfaction. What a job! But I had done it! The wind could blow all it wanted to now. The boat wasn't going anywhere. Nevertheless, I was amazed at how hard the winds were kicking up—amazed, too, that I had weathered the blow and still managed to maneuver the boat safely home.

As I went to work hauling down the sails and making the boat secure, I felt a thrill of triumph. I had sailed in stronger winds than I'd ever dared before. I'd been scared, but I had worked the boat well. I had found my limits and pushed beyond them, and felt now that I could have even done more.

As I waited for the launch to carry me back to the dock, I relished my accomplishment. True, my adventure would probably have been small potatoes for experienced sailors. It wasn't exactly the Vendée Globe Round-the-World Race. I had been out for less than an hour in winds of no more than 25 knots. But the expedition had been my biggest challenge yet, and I had risen to it in fine style. Yes, I thought, I might just be getting the hang of this sailing business.

# 9

# IDYLL WORSHIP

*"Will anyone dare to tell me that business is
more entertaining than fooling among boats?"*
*—Robert Louis Stevenson*

Mostly I sailed alone, and mostly that was fine with me. As long as I was still learning the boat I wanted to make my mistakes in private. I did not relish having my every move corrected and commented on by some wise ass who loved nothing better than showing up the other guy's supposed incompetence. Expert advice was one thing; but in my experience there were more blow-hards than experts in the boating world. Aside from Diego and one or two others, I had not found anyone I trusted enough to witness my bumbling efforts. Besides, trial and error were part of my learning process; if I didn't feel free to screw up I wouldn't learn anything.

As for Ellen, she seemed determined to keep her distance from the boat. Not only did she resist becoming my sailing companion; she fended off every opportunity to come see ADVANCE up close.

"The boat is your thing," she insisted, and despite my pleadings she would not be moved.

The truth was that Ellen had never been fond of boats. Years earlier, newly married and returning from a year abroad, we had crossed the Atlantic in a Danish freighter. Our cabin, though cheap, had been luxurious, the food was first rate and our fellow passengers were congenial. But eight days at sea had stripped away any illusions Ellen may have had about the romance of the sea. For some odd reason she did not enjoy being alternately tossed around in turbulent seas and rolling slowly from side to side on the swells as the ship labored for days at low speed through the encompassing fog.

Nor was she reassured by the stories I brought home from my sailing outings. I could rhapsodize for hours about lovely afternoons spent cruising along on pleasant breezes. I probably should have stopped there, but I couldn't help myself. Coming through the door after my latest adventure, pumped up with adrenaline and excitement, I'd pour out dramatic accounts of battling high winds and whitecaps, or of being stumped by a cranky motor and getting myself back to the mooring by maneuvering—brilliantly! superbly!—under sail alone. Or I'd tell her how, while on a collision course with another boat, my quick thinking and lightning reactions had saved the day.

These were the fun tales to tell: stories of triumph in the face of adversity, heroism in the teeth of danger, lessons learned and skills improved by each exhilarating experience. Unfortunately my yarns had the opposite effect on Ellen. The more exciting the drama, the less enthusiastic she became about ever going near ADVANCE. As far as she could tell, her boat-crazed husband took some sort of twisted pleasure in courting disaster. Now I ask you, what woman in her right mind would want to go out in a boat with a guy like that?

It seemed that I was destined to sail alone—at least until my thrilling afternoons on the water became a little less thrilling.

Which was why I was so delighted when Jesse agreed to come out for a sail during one of his weekend visits.

Since graduating from college, Jesse had been living in New York City, busy with his own life. But every few weeks he would come home to rest up and clean out the refrigerator.

I was always glad to see him, but striking the right balance between friend and father was as tricky as ever. Although I was anxious to keep him close, I knew not to crowd him—knew that if I held on too tight I risked sending him running.

So it was with a certain wariness that I invited him to come out in the boat one afternoon in early August. What I secretly hoped was that he would take to sailing like a duck to water, that he would feel the same passion for it that I did and want to come back for more. What I feared was that he would turn me down—or worse, only say yes because he felt obliged to please his old man.

Was that why he hesitated on Friday night before agreeing to come out with me on Saturday afternoon? Sensing his reluctance, I was all set to backpedal. But then I thought, *To hell with that. He can stand up for himself.* Besides, until he tried sailing he had no way of knowing whether he liked it or not.

It was almost noon on Saturday before he got out of bed, and a couple more hours before he was ready to go out. But by then the weather was perfect. A week of calm, sultry days had left the Hudson lying comatose in its bed, as gray and pasty-faced as an old man after a heart attack. But a storm had swept through on Friday, and by Saturday afternoon there was a nice cool breeze blowing out of the northwest.

Jesse, too, seemed in better spirits. Whatever reluctance he had felt the night before disappeared as soon as we stepped on board.

"It's bigger than I thought," he said approvingly as he let his eye travel up the mast and out to the bow. He poked his head down into the cabin. "A lot of space below, too."

"Go ahead down," I said. "Take a look."

"Uh, no thanks. I think I'll stay up here." Moving tentatively, seeming uncertain about his balance and where to put his feet, he took a seat on the starboard side of the cockpit. But after all, this was his first time on board *any* sailboat. He had a right to be nervous.

I pulled the starter cord on the motor and silently

thanked it when it started up right away. I went forward to cast us off, then came back to the tiller, threw the motor into gear and steered us clear of the mooring field.

"How about taking a turn at the tiller," I offered once we were well beyond the other boats. I was remembering Diego's advice about taking the family out on the water: "Give them something to do so they won't be bored."

At first Jesse demurred. "No, that's all right. I'll just sit here and enjoy the ride."

"Come on, give it a try. It's easy."

"Easy for you," he said.

But he decided to play along and took the tiller. I coached him on how to keep us pointed upriver and he soon got the feel of it. He even began to smile a little.

"This is nice," he said as we slid along on a close reach, the boat leaning slightly.

"Let's follow those guys." I pointed toward two sloops that were a mile or so ahead of us, aiming for the far side of the river. I guessed where they were going: toward the red channel marker that lay in the shadow of a grassy hill on the Westchester shore.

Sure enough, they rounded the buoy, then headed back toward the club.

"This is so nice," Jesse said again after we rounded the buoy.

I reset the sails and we headed back home on a single long tack. The evening was splendid, overcast and a little cool, with the northwest breeze holding nice and steady. And when the sun slipped behind the western hills we had a spectacular light show, the clouds flaring from pale yellow to orange to brilliant pink and purple before fading to gray.

"I can see why you love this," Jesse said. "It really is amazing out here."

I was pleased. He was more relaxed than I had seen him in a long time. For weeks his mind and his gut had been in turmoil as he tried to sort out what might come next in his life—apartment, new job, career plans. Not that he talked much about any of it that evening. In fact, we hardly talked at all, just sailed along enjoying the peace and companionship and the beauty of the river.

With any luck we will have more such times.

August 10th, Saturday:

Is there a rational, step-by-step way to learn this sailing stuff? Or am I doomed to learn everything the hard way?

I went down to the club this morning, hoping to get in a sail before the worst heat of the day. But there was no hint of wind on the water. The river was flat. Rafts of flotsam drifted lazily on the current: tree limbs, odd chunks of lumber, plastic bottles. But no breeze ruffled the surface. We were back to the doldrums again.

A lousy day for sailing, though, meant a perfect day for working on the hull. With that in mind I rode the launch out to ADVANCE, then went below and changed into my swimsuit. Digging around in a storage locker, I came up with Murdock's rope ladder and hung it over the stern. Going forward, I rigged a safety line from a bow cleat, then came back to the cockpit and let myself down the ladder and into the water. I had a plastic paint scraper in my right hand, the floating safety line in my left.

No sooner was I in the water than the current grabbed me, tugging me sternwards. I had expected something like this; that's why I had rigged the safety line. But the strength of the current was a surprise. I wondered what would happen if I lost my grip. Could I make it back to shore before I was carried out to New York Harbor?

Hanging on tight, I pulled myself forward against the current, then set to work, attacking the barnacles on the hull as far below the waterline as I could reach. It was no harder than scraping ice off a car's windshield, except that while I worked I also had to struggle to keep myself afloat. By the time I was done with the starboard side I was already feeling bushed. I should have quit then and there, but I paddled around to the port side and got busy with the scraper again. By the time I had cleared away as many of the barnacles as I could reach I was so tired that I was afraid I would not be able to haul myself back into the boat.

Letting the current carry me back to the stern, I grabbed onto the rope ladder and tried to haul myself up. That's when I discovered how unsuitable the ladder was. It had come with the boat, and presumably Murdock had made use of it. But because of the deep inward curve of the hull, my foot on the bottom rung had nothing to push off against except water. Unable to step up, I had to rely on my arms alone to pull myself up the ladder, and they were already trembling with fatigue. I managed it, but just barely. By the time I scrambled back on board I was thoroughly exhausted, my arms and chest were scraped and sore.

It was a hard way to learn, but learn I did:

1) Next time I go into the water from the boat I will wear a life jacket, never mind how calm the water looks.
2) Next time I will do the scraping and cleaning from a tin boat or from the dock.
3) I need a more useful swim ladder, the stiffened kind that can be permanently fixed to the stern.

I've learned another lesson as well: It's not a good idea to use my bare feet to feel around the bottom of the boat for barnacles. The reason came home to me when I was back in the cockpit, catching my breath and nursing my sore arms and shoulders. That's when I noticed the smears of blood staining my nice white decks. Only then did I realize that my feet and lower legs were badly scraped and cut.

August 11th, Sunday:

A perfect morning for sailing: bright and sunny, with a steady breeze from the northwest. But the wind was blowing directly against the incoming current and the combination had the river in a tumult: whitecaps everywhere, with their tops flinging streamers of mist like mermaids' hair. For myself I had no qualms about going out in such weather. By now I felt confident that I could handle almost anything that the river could throw my way. This morning, though, I would have company: my friend Howard and his younger son, Owen, who is just turning ten. As I stood waiting for them on the launch dock, I wondered if they would be up for such a wild ride. I did not want to push them into something they might regret.

But when they arrived, Howard at least seemed unruffled by the sight of all that white water. "Let's do it," he said. Owen was harder to read. Shy and reticent, he simply shrugged when asked for his opinion. His father seemed willing to interpret that as assent. I hoped he was right. I didn't relish the prospect of sailing with an unhappy crew.

The launch dropped us off at the boat and I got busy coaxing the motor to life while Howard removed the sail cover.

We were just about to cast off when we were hailed by someone calling "Ahoy." I turned to see grinning, red-haired Neil Murdock standing at the helm of his new boat and waving as he came skimming across our stern. His young daughter was with him, her little red-curled head peeping out from over the neck of her orange life vest.

Murdock was in high spirits. Cruising past, he shouted over to us: "I'll stand off until you're ready to go. Meet you out in the river." Then he went flying away.

Murdock's boat was another Tanzer 22. She was trimmed with a red boot stripe instead of a blue one like mine, but in every other way she was identical to ADVANCE.

She'd make a fair competitor in a race and I was eager to test my newly acquired skills.

Ready to go at last, we cast off and headed out to join Murdock. Even reticent young Owen grinned eagerly as we set off in pursuit, and soon we were bearing down on Murdock as he charged through the whitecaps. I managed to catch him, to my great satisfaction and to the keen appreciation of my crew. But then I noticed that his main was flapping; he'd slowed down on purpose to let me catch up. The minute we were on the verge of passing he tightened up his main and went dashing ahead, leaving us lagging behind as though we were standing still.

The difference was in Murdock's daring. While I had the jenny open only half way in order to keep the boat and my passengers upright, Murdock had his genoa full out, which gave him maximum power.

"This sucks," I told Howard. "I don't like looking at his transom, do you?"

"No way."

"Let's get him."

"Go for it."

We eased the jenny out all the way, the boat leaned over, and away we went in a burst of speed.

Powering along in Murdock's wake as we both headed across the wind on a reach, we narrowed the distance between us but could not quite catch him. But when we reached the shipping channel he turned downwind toward the bridge and that's when we caught up to him.

"You've been doing some sailing," he shouted over to me as we slipped alongside then pulled ahead.

"You bet!" I called back, thumb in the air. What I did not say was that I had also just scraped the boat's bottom so it was nice and slick. But why spoil a compliment with such mundane technical details? I was one proud skipper!

Later in the morning, after Murdock peeled off and headed back downstream to his mooring on the other side of

the bridge, I had the pleasure of standing in "the pit"—
halfway down the cabin steps—and giving orders to my
crew, then watching as they went to work, with Owen at the
tiller and holding us nicely on course.

What a wonderful day. We could have stayed out for
hours yet. The great river was our playground. Stretching
out and away to the north and south, it beckoned us to new
adventures. Twenty-five miles to the south lay New York
Harbor: the magnificent skyline, the great cruise ships coming and going, the Statue of Liberty. To the north we could
sail across the broad expanse of Haverstraw Bay, then thread
our way between the lofty, wooded hills of the Highlands.

The tide was favorable for a northward run. Given
enough time we might even make it to Cold Spring. A picturesque riverside village tucked at the base of the mountains
near the northern end of the Highlands, Cold Spring was a
favorite destination for Nyack cruisers. But it was twenty-
five miles away, a five-hour trip, and we were already running out of time. At home, spouses and families waited.
Obligations. Schedules. Commitments.

"We better turn back," I told my crew.

"Aw. Do we have to?" asked Owen.

"Afraid so. As it is, it'll take us at least an hour to get
back to the mooring."

As Owen dutifully pointed us back west and Howard
reset the sails, I silently salved my own regret by reminding
myself again about the importance of keeping things in balance in this boating game. Family, boat, work—spend too
much time on any one of the three and you risked capsizing
the other two.

Our sailing time may have been brief, but it was far from
being a loss. I had enjoyed a fine couple of hours of companionship and shared excitement. But there was another
bonus as well: the seed of a new dream had been planted in
my brain. I was now determined to take the boat on an

overnight trip to Cold Spring. One way or another I would not let this summer go by without it. After all, why own a boat with beds in it if not to go voyaging beyond my own back yard?

August 19th, Monday:
I missed sailing this past weekend. As someone once said, "It had priority but other things came first." Instead of sailing, I flew to Wisconsin for a family visit, combined with a book-signing at a local bookstore. No sooner did I get back home than Ellen went into the hospital for gall bladder surgery. Sailing had to wait.

Still, there were always boat things to be done, and after the hubbub of my Wisconsin visit and my worries about Ellen's surgery, anything I could do around the boat was likely to be therapeutic.

The task this time was to prepare the new tiller I had bought for ADVANCE: a gracefully formed, yard-long handle of unfinished oak and teak laminate. True, the old tiller still did the basic job of steering the boat, but it looked faded and splintery. It offended my eye and it offended my pride. I wanted my little boat to look its best.

Picking up my toolbox, I carried it down to the club and took myself out to ADVANCE. There, while bobbing at the mooring, I unbolted the old tiller from the rudder, then carried it back home, where I laid it out on my basement work-bench beside the new model.

I intended to use the bolt holes of the old tiller as my guide when drilling the new one. The new holes had to line up precisely with the metal brackets by which the tiller attached to the rudder. But as I studied the fine, expensive piece of new wood, I grew increasingly nervous. I didn't want to botch the job, yet all I had to work with was a cheap little hand drill—a thirty-year-old hand-me-down from my father's tool kit. I didn't even have a vise to hold the wood steady. If the holes were off by even a sixteenth of an inch the brackets would not line up correctly and I'd have ruined the new tiller. I needed better equipment.

"Do you know anyone with a drill press?" I asked Jesse. He had come home to visit Ellen in the hospital. Now, before heading back to the city, he had joined me for an after-dinner walk.

Unfortunately no one he knew had the kind of machinery I needed. As we walked on, though, we met a friend of mine who was out strolling with his wife. We stopped long enough to say hello and I asked him the same question I had asked Jesse. No, he said, he did not have a drill press. But he thought our mutual friend, Howard, might have one.

"Great," I said. "Thanks for the tip."

Suddenly I couldn't wait to get home and get to the phone.

When I called, though, all I got was Howard's answering machine. "Damn it," I said as I slammed down the receiver. My nice relaxing boat project was turning into another frustration.

"Is there a problem?" Jesse asked.

"He's not home."

"Can't it wait?"

"No," I barked. "It can't."

Jesse looked startled. "Hey, I'm just asking."

His reaction brought me up short. Why was I getting so worked up? Of course the project could wait. I just didn't want it to.

"Sorry," I said. "I guess I'm getting a little obsessive."

"I guess," he said, and tactfully refrained from saying more.

Only later did I realize why I was getting so nutty about that tiller, why I wanted so badly to do the job right then, right that minute. With so much else out of my hands—Ellen in the hospital; my book out in the stores and awaiting reviews and sales figures; chaos at my office, where the staff was being decimated by layoffs and reorganizations—I was desperate to take hold of at least this one small thing, this elegant stick of wood, make it right and make it work. I needed to get some corner of my life back on course.

August 22nd, Thursday:
Spent an hour yesterday evening hunting down a drill press. A few calls to friends around town led me to Dan, a local carpenter, who invited me to drop by after supper.

His house still smelled of pot roast, peppers and onions when I came through the door. But as Dan led me downstairs to his basement workshop the air became fragrant with wood shavings and machine oil. The spacious, well-lit room included an array of equipment that would have been the envy of any woodworker: a large table saw, a lathe, a couple of workbenches, pegboards hung with an impressive array of hand tools.

While Dan oiled up his drill press and found the right bit, I carefully aligned the new tiller alongside the old and bound them tightly side by side with duct tape. Next, Dan lined up the drill bit over the guide holes in the old tiller, flicked the "On" switch, and brought the bit down carefully once, twice, three times. In less than a minute the job was done.

"That's great," I said, examining my new tiller handle. "What do I owe you?"

He waved me off. "Forget it. Just give me a call sometime when you need crew."

"It's a deal."

Back home I fitted the brackets to the new tiller and slipped in the bolts. The last of the three holes was off by a hair, but all it took was a few taps of a hammer and the bolt slid home. A perfect fit! It was a small but comforting conclusion amid the tumult and uncertainty that dogs the rest of my life these days.

August 24th, Saturday:
Summer doldrums. Hardly a whiff of wind these past few days. The heat and humidity have been awful. The river is smooth as a mirror. Boats and their reflections shimmer in air that is half water. Not promising for sailing, but I tried anyway. The season is almost over and I want to grab every minute I can out on the river. The good news is that Ellen is home from the hospital and recovering well from her operation. But she spends a lot of time sleeping, so today I was able to get away to the boat for a few hours without feeling conflicted.

I got lucky. When I raised the sail a slight breeze carried me off the mooring. But it lasted just long enough to push me clear of the other boats, then dropped again, leaving me drifting with the current, sails flapping idly. I dawdled along for a while, hoping for another breeze, just a puff, anything. The sun got hotter by the minute. In the thick air the traffic on the bridge, two miles away, roared like Niagara. Across the river a souped-up powerboat came blasting up the channel, its bow raised high, its business end digging into the water and sending up a rooster tail that was bigger than the boat itself. So much for my vision of a peaceful morning of boating.

Grumpy and hot, I motored back to the mooring and tied up. But I wasn't ready to go back to my shore life just yet. Just sitting there at the mooring felt like a little vacation.

I busied myself tidying up the cabin, then strung up a spare sail for an awning and sat on the deck with needle and thread and repaired a tear in the sail cover. It wasn't as much fun as sailing, but it was better than anything else I could think of doing just now.

August 29th, Thursday:
The breezes are back, the river stirring in its bed, especially late in the day, when the land starts cooling off. It made for perfect sailing last night, when I went out with Howard and

his older son, Jake, a bright and funny eleven-year-old who is as outgoing and talkative as his brother is shy and reticent.

We started off by chasing around the buoys that marked the course for the Wednesday-night racers. The course, a triangle, was laid out in a little cove just upriver from the bridge. The racers—heavy-bottomed Ensigns and frisky Thistles—darted from buoy to buoy and crowded each other in the turns, and we could tell from the cheers and catcalls that they were having a great time squeezing each other out: the sailor's equivalent of a thumb in the eye.

The tight quarters made me nervous. I didn't want to get in the way and I certainly didn't want my nice white hull to get bumped and scraped by some psyched up skipper. So I headed upstream, where we could see four or five cruising boats running in loose formation toward a distant channel marker. They were well ahead of us, but we seemed to have a better breeze than they did, or maybe they weren't really trying, because little by little we began to catch up.

After an hour or so of hot pursuit, we began to close in on the big sloop that was in the rear of the formation. Rising high out of the water, with a black band around her middle, she looked like a miniature version of an old British man-o'-war—the kind of ship sailed by Captain Horatio Hornblower himself. She even had gunports, or seemed to. When we got closer, we could see the ports were no more than a painted illusion. Still, the look of that boat was enough to inspire us with piratical fantasies.

"Let's send a shot across her transom," Howard suggested as we crept up on the warship in the fading light.

"Good idea, Mr. Andrews," I said. "Ensign, prepare the guns."

"Aye aye, sir," Jake said.

"And if she doesn't stop we'll give her one below her waterline."

"We'll blow her out of the water!"

We finally pulled abreast of the bigger but slower boat.

With the wind fading, I enjoy a dramatic sunset as I head home after a lively evening sail on the Tappan Zee. *Photo by Chris Bowser*

Cupping my hands, I shouted over to their skipper: "Send over your grog or we'll board you."

A burst of laughter came out of the twilight from the sloop's skipper and crew. The reaction aboard ADVANCE was even more enthusiastic. Jacob laughed and laughed as though our little game was the funniest thing he had ever heard. Or maybe he was just surprised to discover that even grownups can be silly.

The light was almost gone by the time we turned for home. The darkness closed in, and soon the only way we knew there were other boats around us was by the red and green running lights we saw gliding along in the darkness and by the muffled voices that drifted our way. Sometimes, too, we'd see the faint shadow of a sail ghosting across the lights that shone on the far shore.

Overhead, the top of our mast swayed across a sky full of stars, the constellations flung across the heavens like fairy dust—guiding lights to those who know how to read them. Looking up, I could only wonder how it is done, and I promised myself that one day I would take a course in celestial navigation. I'd love to know the secret. And who knows? Someday it might help me find my way across the ocean.

But it was conversation more than contemplation that interested young Jacob. He chattered away, seemingly unimpressed by the display overhead and by the quiet beauty of the evening. But then the unexpected happened. Quite suddenly and mysteriously, a slice of orange light winked up over the eastern hills.

"Look," I said, pointing.

Even Jacob was moved to awe. "What is it?" he breathed.

"Watch," I said.

The orange slice began to swell, growing larger and fatter as it rose from behind the hill where it had been hiding, growing first to a quarter circle, then to a half. It was like watching a huge basketball being pumped up, and it seemed to be happening so fast that you could almost trace the movement with your eye.

A few minutes more and the rising moon became a nearly full circle. Only the bottom edge still clung to the hilltop. Then that edge, too, popped free, as if someone had cut its tether to the earth. Rising majestically into the sky, the enormous globe set a golden pathway shimmering on the water, leading right to our boat.

"Wow!" Jacob said, his voice hushed.

"Boy, you said it," whispered his father.

In prayerful silence we sat. Nor did we hear any more voices from other boats. It was as if the whole world was holding its breath.

I could have stayed out forever in that magical light. But it was already after nine, the wind was dying, and if we didn't put the motor on, we'd be out here for hours. I pulled the starter cord, furled the genoa, put the motor in gear and steered for home.

As we headed back, we ghosted past the dark silhouette of a larger boat, its running light showing green on its starboard bow. The murmur of voices drifted toward us across the dark water.

Feeling a mellow camaraderie with our fellow idlers, I called out a greeting: "Gorgeous evening," I said.

"Wonderful," replied a husky male voice out of the darkness.

"Too bad we have to get up early and go to work tomorrow," I added.

A note of smug triumph accompanied the reply: "Not us," said the voice. "We're all retired."

Howard's groan of self-pity echoed my own. At that moment our eyes must have shown as green in the night as the light on the other boat's bow.

# 10

# FULL CIRCLE

*"Come, my friends,*
*"Tis not too late to seek a newer world."*
*—Alfred Lord Tennyson, "Ulysses"*

Sunsets came earlier each day. Summer was slipping away, taking the sailing season with it. I felt a pang of impending loss. ADVANCE had been part of the rhythm of my life ever since I had first seen the "For Sale" flier in the window of the Community Market. Since then, the boat and the river had become woven into the fabric of my daily life in ways I had never expected. Far from loosening their grip on my imagination as the season progressed, they occupied my thoughts and dreams more than ever. Familiarity had bred not contempt but heightened passion.

Each time I slipped the mooring I felt a surge of delight. The tricks of current and weather; the trim of the sails; the quiet joy of an easy outing in a fair wind; the thrill of riding a rising blow and knowing, really knowing, what the boat and I could do together—I could imagine no better antidote to the predictable routines of an otherwise well-ordered life.

The truth was, life ashore held precious few challenges these days. My editorial work continued to be interesting and I was paid well for my efforts, but after almost twenty years at the same job I can't say I woke up each morning with a fire in my belly, lusting to seize the next corporate opportunity.

Home, in turn, meant comfort and security, and for that I felt enormously grateful. With so many marriages crumbling around us, and so many friends becoming suddenly single, I came home at night to a woman who was still friend and lover after almost thirty years of marriage. We enjoyed each other's company, had fun, fought now and then, and continued to support one another's dreams and aspirations.

All of this was wonderful. I had absolutely no reason to complain. My life was blessed. But was it too good? Why else would I feel this vague sense of discontent? Something was missing: the gift of surprise, of elation, of excitement. Hardly ever was I brought up short by awe, or by fear, or by the thrill of a new experience. Hardly ever did I have a chance to see the world with new eyes and with a sense of eager anticipation.

That's where the boat came in. On the water there were mysteries I was only now beginning to fathom: secrets of an ancient and elemental knowledge going back thousands of years: to Odysseus and the Phoenicians; to Eric the Red and Columbus; to Magellan, Hudson, Drake, Cook and that whole grand brotherhood of adventurers who dared uncharted seas and discovered places never seen before.

Not that I expected to make any such epic voyage. But now, with growing confidence in myself and my boat, I could imagine sailing down the coast to, say, Chesapeake Bay or up the coast to Maine. Some day I might even brave wider seas, perhaps the Atlantic itself!

For now, though, the Hudson was New World enough, and I savored every opportunity to learn the lessons it had to teach.

September 1st, Sunday:
My longest cruise yet: a full day on the river. I had been hoping for an overnight, and had been tempted to join Murdock and his friend who was also co-owner of his boat. They left early yesterday morning for a trip upriver to Cold Spring. But Ellen still wasn't feeling a hundred percent after her operation and I didn't want to be away for that long. A day trip would do nicely.

The sky was milky overcast. A light breeze blew from the northeast, giving a lift to the racing fleets that dotted the river behind me as I sailed away from the club. On the far shore another group of racers was getting started, their clustered sails looking like a collection of teepees. It was a great day to be out.

I tacked upriver against the current, staying as close to the wind as possible. I was hoping to get to the bay behind Croton Point, about five miles upriver from the club, where there is a nice sheltered anchorage. But the river gods had other ideas. The winds were too light and the downstream current too strong for me to make much headway, so I readjusted my plans. Rounding the channel marker off the Westchester shore—the one Jesse and I had played tag with a few weeks ago—I tacked back northwest, heading for the broad reaches of Haverstraw Bay.

I was halfway across when it occurred to me that Murdock and his buddy would probably be on their way back from their Cold Spring trip just about now. I wondered if I'd spot them.

Sure enough, not fifteen minutes later I saw, in the distance, the distinctive size and shape of their Tanzer. With its rakish lines, its red boot stripe and the red trim on the clew of the genoa, there wasn't another boat like it on the river.

I gave a wave and saw them wave in return, then change course to head in my direction. As they closed, I swung about and adjusted speed until I matched their heading. They soon caught up and slipped into position beside me. With no more than ten feet separating our hulls, conversation was easy. Murdock and his buddy filled me in on their journey: where they had anchored, what conditions they had encountered, their sightings of bald eagles and egrets.

"Sounds terrific," I shouted back. "I wish I'd been there."

"We'll do it again. I'll let you know when. Maybe we can team up."

We sailed and talked together a while longer, then parted company. With a wave, they headed back downriver and I turned north and west. As the distance increased between us, I understood a little of how ocean sailors must feel after meeting other boats during long, lonely voyages: happy for the company, but happy, too, to be on their own again.

By this time I had been out on the river for over two hours, and what I wanted now was to find a quiet place to drop anchor and take a breather. I also wanted to practice anchoring. Although I had helped out a couple of times during my classes with Diego, I had never tried doing it on my own. It was time I learned.

Where to go? I was trying to edge north, up the bay, but the breeze had shifted and was now coming at me almost directly from the direction I was trying to go. Wind and current were combining to push me more west than north. Reluctantly I concluded that unless I wanted to spend a lot more hours and energy than I had to spare, I was not likely to make any further headway upstream.

All right, I'd resort to Hudson River Rule #1: Go with the flow. I'd head for the western shore, where the cliffs of the Palisades rise abruptly from the river's edge. I knew that shore, had hiked its footpaths many times and had seen boats anchored in the small coves that were tucked in beneath the cliffs. If they could do it, so could I.

I cruised along the shore until I found the perfect spot: no fishermen, no other boats nearby. Nor did I see any hikers or mountain-bikers among the trees that lined the shore. If there were any, they'd likely be higher up on the slope, along the main path. As far as I could tell I had the whole neighborhood to myself.

Now to set the anchor. With the wind pushing me toward the shore, I realized that maneuvering into position under sail would be the hard way, and probably not the safest. Using the motor would give me better control in case something went wrong. I certainly did not want to end up on those rocks that jutted from the shore.

I started the motor, dropped the sails, and motored cautiously toward shallow water. I was wary of getting in too close. The chart gave the depth here as ten to twelve feet, and with my three-and-a-half-foot draft I had plenty of water under me. But I also knew that the bottom rose very quickly closer to shore. Better to play it safe and stand off a bit.

Once I felt I was close enough, I set the engine to idle, then quickly went forward, broke out the anchor, secured the anchor line to a bow cleat, and dropped the hook over the side, easing the chain down until I felt it go slack as it touched bottom. I played out a good bit of line, then went back to the motor, kicked it into reverse, and slowly backed down from the anchor until I felt it catch and hold. Tah-dah! Success!

Smiling to myself at yet another small triumph, I checked the position of a willow on shore to make sure the anchor wasn't dragging. Only then did I allow myself a sigh of relief. I had completed my first solo anchoring and I was safe and sound. It was a small thing, but as I had been learning all summer, a lot of these small things were adding up to improved skills.

I thought of getting out the swim ladder and rewarding myself with a nice cool dip in the river. But I had second thoughts. I remembered how hard it had been to clamber back aboard after my over-the-side effort at hull cleaning. I also remembered how strong the current had been. I certainly did not want to get swept away from the boat. Even with a safety line hung over the side, I was reluctant to risk it. If I got into trouble no one was around to help me out. Better to just relax, enjoy what I had and where I was.

I stripped to shorts and bare feet, then broke out my lunch bag from the freezer chest. Sitting there in the sun, I feasted on a cheese sandwich and an apple while enjoying the best view of the Hudson that any restaurant had to offer:

a sweeping vista of blue water, milky sky and distant hills. Behind me, in the forest, birds called back and forth, their voices echoing among the trees.

This perfect idyll lacked only one thing, and I proceeded to make it my next order of business. After checking to make sure the anchor was holding fast, I went below, pulled the hatch cover shut to block out the sun, stretched out on the quarter berth, then closed my eyes and let the gentle rocking of the river lull me to sleep.

Some time later a buzzing sound began playing around the edge of my consciousness, intruding on my dreams of a tropical paradise. Flies? No, this was something else, and it was getting louder.

Dragging myself back to wakefulness, I sat up, shoved back the hatch cover, and stuck my head up into the sunshine just in time to see two high-speed powerboats go racing by less than a hundred yards away, kicking up huge wakes. Damn, I thought, isn't there any place on this river where you can get away from the racket of machinery?

As I braced for the wakes, I glanced at my watch. Oh, well. It was almost two o'clock anyway. Time to start back.

Still groggy from my nap, I donned shoes and shirt, got the motor started, then went forward and upped anchor. It was much heavier coming up than it was going down, and when it finally broke the surface I saw why. Stuck to its flukes was a thick gray pudding of river muck. I made an effort to scrape it clean but there was no time. I was adrift now, and unless I got back to the tiller quickly and motored off, I risked running aground. Safety would have to take precedence over tidiness. Into the hatch went the muddy hook and a chaotic tangle of chain. I'd sort the mess out later. First things first. Back to the cockpit I went, threw the motor into gear and headed out into open water.

The breeze had come up nicely during my nap, and as

soon as I was well clear of the shore I raised the sails, killed the motor and set off on a fast downriver run. The wind got stronger by the minute until I was fairly flying. By the time I was within shouting distance of the mooring field I was pounding through whitecaps.

I was tempted to stay out and do some fast upwind sailing. I was like a kid in an amusement park: overexcited and not wanting to quit. But my head and my body were telling me that I'd had enough for one day. Conditions were getting worse, the waves wilder and more confused by the minute. I knew why: another hurricane was moving up the coast and this was part of the storm surge. If I stayed out much longer I'd be in for a good bashing.

I sailed up to the mooring, grabbed it on the first pass and got the boat tied down. Quickly I cleared the decks, locked up the cabin, secured the tiller and the jib sheets, then got on the radio and called for the launch.

I arrived back on shore tired but happy. My first extended day of cruising rated an A+. I had handled the boat and the weather well. I had also taken on two new tests toward mastery and passed them with flying colors: anchoring and napping. At last I could consider myself fully qualified for an overnight.

September 9th, Monday:

Got up early yesterday morning and hurried down to the club to check on the boat. Last week's hurricane hit us only a glancing blow and did little damage, but the wind had blown long and hard and I was anxious to see how ADVANCE had fared.

It was still early when I got down to the club—just past eight. But I was not early enough to beat Morris. I shouldn't have been surprised. Morris is a regular wharf rat. He spends more time at the club than anyone else and seems to have a hand in everything, whether it's sailing his 28-foot cruiser, crewing in races, repairing club equipment or raking the lawn. He claims to have a job as an elevator engineer, but it's hard to tell how he can hold down a job and still spends so much time at the club.

When I arrived at the dock, I found him there, revving up one of the tin boats for a run out to his sloop. Helpful as ever, he offered to ferry me out to ADVANCE.

Dark-haired, bearded and olive-skinned, Morris is the opposite of the silent, introspective sailor. He is exuberant, quick with a joke and has a gift for hospitality that must be inherited from his Syrian ancestors. I have never seen him happier than when he is hosting a boatload of people, the more the merrier. One evening not long ago, seeing his boat tied up at the end of the dock with what looked like a large crowd of people sitting or standing in the cockpit, I went over to say hello and found him entertaining no less than eight guests, all of them sipping beer or rum-and-coke and having a good time, Morris most of all. The cockpit was standing room only, but he did not hesitate to invite me to the join the party. Happy to accept, I found a seat on the cabin top, popped a beer, and stayed late.

Self-schooled as a sailor, Morris is never shy about sharing his knowledge or advising the rest of us on how to improve our vessels or our skills. Sometimes this can be annoying.

"Morris, you're right," I heard one skipper retort after being told how to trim his own sails. "And I hate it when you're right."

But Morris knows his stuff and I have often been grateful for his suggestions. Whether he is showing me how to tweak more power from the mainsail or how to tie off my halyards so they don't get tangled, his advice is almost always on the money. And as eager as he is to offer his opinion, he is equally quick to lend a hand. Shuttling me out to ADVANCE yesterday was just like him. If I had asked him to come back in two hours to pick me up, I'm sure he would have cheerfully done that, too.

To my relief, ADVANCE looked no worse for wear from the hurricane's backlash. I saw no chaffing on the mooring lines, no bent fittings and no scrapes on the hull from passing debris. My little boat had been lucky again.

I hoisted sail, cast off the lines, and let the wind take me. The morning was overcast, but very beautiful. A scrim of bright mist hung behind the bridge, so that the metal superstructure looked as if it had been etched on soft paper with a fine-tipped pencil.

The tide had just reached slack-before-ebb, which meant the current would be against me on the way back up river. But the wind was favorable for a downstream run, and I was drawn on by that magical light silhouetting the bridge. Threading my way beneath it and back again would be fun. All my recent voyages had taken me upriver. I was ready for a new view, a new challenge.

Wary as ever of the busy main channel with its barge and freighter traffic, I aimed instead for one of the small side channels between the concrete bridge abutments. The wind kept shifting and pushing me off course, though, and I knew that under the bridge, where the giant supports interrupted the air flow, the wind would be even more erratic. This pass-through maneuver was going to be tricky.

With the wind coming straight up the river, I had to come at the opening from an oblique angle. Running almost parallel to the bridge, I was able to sneak part way under, but then found myself headed directly for the massive abutment on the opposite side. I got as close as I dared, then did a quick tack back in the opposite direction, where I now found myself headed for the opposite piling. Once again I got as close as I dared, fighting for every foot of progress down river. If I hit that concrete abutment I'd be lucky if the only damage was a bad scrape to the hull. A hole and a sinking were more likely.

While the traffic roared overhead, I crept up to the abutment—careful, careful, just a little closer—then tacked away

ADVANCE and I skirt the shipping channel just north of the Tappan Zee Bridge. Barge and ship traffic, combined with erratic wind shifts caused by the bridge superstructure, can make sailing under the bridge a tricky proposition. *Photo by Chris Bowser*

at the last minute from the looming concrete wall. The genoa flapped wildly as the sheets spun out through the blocks. Sweat dripped off my forehead and into my eyes. But as I sheeted the genoa in again and started back on my new tack, I saw that I had gained a few yards of headway and was now halfway under the bridge.

It took all my concentration to manage it, and more than once I felt panicky as I struggled with the tangled sheets. But after a few more tacks I came through the gap without a scratch and sailed out into the broad open river below the bridge.

It surprised me how different the river looked on the downriver side of the bridge. Visually and psychologically the bridge acts as a barrier between my world and the broader world beyond. Passing beneath it and coming out on the other side, I felt as if I had passed through a gateway. Nothing now stood between me and New York Harbor, the Atlantic Ocean, and the exhilarating promise of endless freedom. I yearned to keep going. One day I will, too—when I know more and have more time. I'll follow the river and the wind to wherever they carry me.

Not yet, though. Yesterday I was on a short tether. Ellen and I had promised to visit friends in the afternoon. As usual my sailing time was limited to a few hours snatched from a busy life.

Still, I was determined to make the most of the time I had. It was a gift after all and no less precious for being a small one.

Turning west, I headed toward the place where Murdock moored his boat. Was he watching from his hillside house? Would he come out to play?

As if in answer, a sail appeared near shore. From this distance I could not tell if it was Murdock, but I kept heading his way even as he came toward me.

Eventually the other boat got close enough for me to see that it was missing that distinctive red stripe around the gunwales. Not Murdock then. Still, the boat was about the same size as mine, and seemed to have roughly the same sail area. This looked promising. We might just have some fun together.

As our boats closed, we acknowledged one another with a wave, and when we were at last parallel, I swung ADVANCE around and put myself on his heading. He was clipping along nicely and I worked to match his pace and even to pass him if I could.

And just like that we were racing. I had to smile. Yes, it was true what people said: Get two boats together on the water and you've got a race.

The newcomer was heading up toward the bridge and the mid-channel opening, which was perfect since I needed to start for home anyway. We played tag for a while, matching each other's tacks, silently adjusting the set of our sails, reaching for optimum power and efficiency. Whoever he was, he was giving me a run for my money.

What a pretty sight we must have made for the people passing overhead in their cars and trucks and busses: our two boats leaning into the wind, skimming the waves like a pair of gulls.

We passed beneath the bridge at exactly the same time, our race a draw. I was pleased. I had done well, kept up and not been left behind. The only thing better would have been an outright win.

Then, with another wave, we went our separate ways. He continued upriver while I turned back west toward the club. We had been strangers when we met and were strangers when we parted. We had not exchanged a word. But for a few moments on this one small corner of the planet our two lives had intersected and we had shared the joy of a beautiful, bountiful day.

September 13th, Friday:
Time to think about where I'll store ADVANCE for the winter. Today I called a couple of marinas to find out their rates.

Storing the boat at the club would be my best bet. The cost in dollars per foot is half of what I'd be charged at a marina. But to store it at the club I'd need to spend hundreds of dollars to buy a cradle and I am already way over my boat budget for the year. Also, I'll need to take the mast down so I can fix the head light and the radio antenna, both of which are on the fritz. And dropping the mast is not a job that I am ready to tackle on my own. Better to leave such things to the pros, at least for now.

I hate thinking about all this. ADVANCE and I have had such a wonderful season together. I am not ready for it to be over.

September 15th, Sunday:
Feeling like company for a change, rather than solitude, I invited Howard and his older son, Jacob, out for a sail this morning. Our last outing had been so much fun—our piratical twilight chase after that other boat; the quiet awe of seeing that orange moon creeping up the sky above the eastern hills—that I was eager for another boyish adventure with the two of them.

But I regretted the impulse almost immediately. A busy wind was churning the river to froth and when the launch pulled up alongside ADVANCE, the boat was pitching and heaving so wildly that it was an adventure just getting aboard.

"You okay?" I asked Jacob after I'd helped him over the gunwales.

Far from being intimidated by the whistling wind and the tossing deck, he just laughed and spread his arms wide. "I love it!" he crowed.

His bravado worried me, though, especially when he reached into his lunch bag and pulled out an ersatz breakfast of peanut butter sandwiches on white bread. While Howard got the cover off the mainsail and I coaxed the outboard to life, the fair-haired lad sat there quite happily stuffing his face. It was not hard to guess what would come next. But I didn't say anything. He wasn't my kid. If he was going to be sick it was between him and his father.

Sure enough, by the time we cast off Jake's grin was gone and pink cheeks had taken on a pukey hue.

"How are you doing?" his father asked.

"I think I better go back," he moaned.

"Aw, come on, you'll get over it," I said.

"I'd hate to make a mess of your boat," Jake warned.

Blackmail! From a ten-year old!

"Just make sure you do it over the downwind side," I replied. I was really ticked off. I didn't want my afternoon held hostage by a queasy kid.

Fortunately, though, Jake's pride proved stronger than his stomach. When his threat proved ineffective, he took matters into his own hands. Scrambling forward in search of fresh air, he settled himself astride the bow with his feet dangling just inches above the tossing waves.

I probably should have called him back. I discovered later that it was against Coast Guard safety rules for anyone to ride up there, especially young kids. But Jake had on a life jacket and he seemed tucked securely inside the bow pulpit, so I let him stay. "Just make sure you hang on tight," I called up to him.

It turned out to be the perfect prescription for what ailed him. Before long he was whooping and laughing as we ran briskly across the river, dashing through the whitecaps, spray flying off the bow and soaking him good. He loved every minute.

Reaching the shipping lane, we swung down river and headed for the bridge. The west wind carried us under on a perfect beam reach, with none of the in-your-face struggle that I had endured a few days ago. And there again was that wonderful view opening before us: the river calling us on toward New York Harbor and the wide world beyond. Savoring the sight, Howard and I shared the same impulse.

"Hey, I've got fifteen dollars," I said. "Let's see how far we can get before we have to stop and work for more money."

"Great!" Howard grinned. "We'll head for the Caribbean."

"Let's do it."

Too bad it was nothing but talk. No wild and crazy stunts for us. Instead, we sailed on a little further, then turned back for home, where obligations waited. That's just our problem: we are both too damned sensible for our own good. We need a flaky buddy, someone who will get us to do something really insane.

September 19th, Thursday:

The season is winding down, at least for the racing fleets. Last night was the last of the Wednesday night races and I went down to the club to watch the fun while sailing around on my own. It has been a hectic week at home and at the office and I was looking forward to spending some time alone on the boat to clear my head. But at the dock I ran into a guy I knew, an avid racer named Al, who asked if he could join me. His own boat needed repair and all the other racing boats had full crew, so he was glad for the chance to get into the race.

"Sure, come on," I said, not wanting to be unsociable. Besides, I thought I might learn something.

It was the right thing to do. Al not only knew the race rules and how to run the course; he also gave me some useful strategy tips. And he got his lessons across without being obnoxious about it.

"Do you know this?" he'd ask before explaining some point of boat handling. A kindergarten teacher for thirty years, he knew how to teach without being condescending. The kids must love him. He's easy going, humorous, but also clear and direct—a great combination.

A pair of Lightnings were the only boats on the line at the

start of the race and they darted around ADVANCE as if we were standing still. But the competition kept things interesting. As we worked our way around the course, Al handled the sheets while I manned the tiller.

"Sail the tell-tales," he coached, indicating the little strips of tape that fluttered from the forward edge of the foresail, green on the starboard side, red to port. When these streamed straight back we could be certain we were on the best tack for fast and efficient sailing. I recalled having heard the same advice from Diego, but there had been so much else to learn in those early days that I had been unable to absorb it all.

September 22nd, Sunday:
Going out to the boat today, I discovered that I had made a nearly fatal mistake the other night, when I was out with Al.

We had arrived back at the mooring just as the light was fading and the launch was making its last round to take people off their boats. Hurrying so as not to miss the launch or keep the others waiting, Al and I quickly battened everything down, then got ready to disembark. I was just about to follow Al off the boat when I noticed that the gas line was still hooked up to the motor.

"Hang on a sec," I said. "I forgot something."

Reaching back, I popped the fuel line off the outboard, stowed it in the lazarette and closed the lid. Then I stepped off onto the launch.

What I didn't realize was that in my hurry I very nearly caused the kind of disaster I read about in the boating magazines.

Normally whenever I disconnect the fuel line I wrap it around the top of the gas can, where the nozzle is elevated. The other night I cut corners, carelessly letting the nozzle fall to the bottom of the lazarette. By the time I returned to the boat today, enough gas had leaked out into the hold to send a wave of fumes into my face as soon as I opened the hatch.

I hate to think what would have happened if I'd been a smoker and opened that hatch with a lighted cigarette dangling from my fingers. Bye-bye boat, and me with it. Instead I received a life-saving lesson. There are good reasons for keeping a boat shipshape—in Bristol trim, as the saying goes. Efficiency is one reason. Safety is another.

September 24th, Tuesday:
Seeing Howard's sons in town yesterday, I felt my heart swell with affection for the two of them. As my own sailing experiences multiply and I begin to take the boat for granted, all I have to do is recall their boyish delight during the times we sailed together. I remember Jacob's laughter when, perched on the pitching bow and hanging on for dear life, he seemed to overflow with joy. And I remember Owen's delight as we went chasing after Murdock and managed to catch him. Seeing these things through their young eyes, feeling them through their young hearts, I am reminded of the pleasures that brought me to sailing in the first place.

September 30th, Monday:
Little sailing this past month. Too much going on in the rest of my life: work, family, social obligations, religious holidays, home repairs, yard work. An occasional quick trip to the clubhouse is about all I've been able to manage: a few minutes stolen on the way home from the hardware or the grocery store just so I can stand on the clubhouse porch and gaze out at ADVANCE through binoculars. Just the sight of her filled me with yearning.

This past Saturday, though, I finally had a free afternoon and I was psyched up at the prospect of a lively sail. Even Ellen felt stirred by my enthusiasm and for a while it seemed as if she might join me. But she shied away at the last minute.

"You should have something you do yourself," she said.

I wasn't sure whether she was being generous or just

looking for an excuse to stay off the boat. But I was too impatient to stay and find out. I collected my gear, grabbed a water bottle and a bag of snacks, then hurried away.

Even before I got to the club I could tell that sailing today was going to be lively. The treetops were flailing wildly in the wind. Conditions out on the river would be nothing less than hair-raising.

Sure enough, when I got down to club, the Hudson was tossing furiously, boats straining at their moorings like stallions eager to be let loose to run. I watched, torn between wanting to sail and the fear of what I'd face if I did. The wind was howling. Down at the pier the river had the floating finger docks in its teeth and was shaking them like a dog shaking a rag, making them creak and jump on their cables.

I pulled on a life vest, then stood on the pier, trying to decide what to do. Ted, the launch operator, waited, ready to ferry me out to the boat if that's what I wanted. But did I? I saw no sails on the river. Mine would be the first. But would that be smart? It's one thing to get caught in a blow; it's another to go plunging into it on purpose.

I had no doubt that the boat could handle it, and I felt confident that I could too. If I used the bare minimum of sail—just a sliver of the genoa—I could keep the boat upright, no problem. It would be good, scary fun. What worried me most was the prospect of getting the boat back onto the mooring when I was done. That was a battle I was not sure I could win.

"What do you think?" I asked Ted. "It looks like it's blowing twenty or twenty-five."

"Oh, at least," he said, tightening the collar on his foul-weather jacket. "I'll bet the gusts are up to thirty-five."

A thick-set, big-bellied guy who sounded gruffer than he was, Ted had been around boats most of his life, including, I think, a stint in the navy. Since he was now into his late sixties, all those years on the water added up to plenty of experience. If anyone was a good judge of sea conditions it would be him. But he was offering no advice, letting me decide.

I waffled a while longer, chewing my lip while I watched the waves tossing the boats and pounding the docks. Finally I made up my mind. "I guess I'll bag it," I said.

"Good call," Ted replied. "You wouldn't get me out in that."

I felt better, having my judgment confirmed. Still, it was frustrating to turn my back on the one chance I've had for weeks to get out on the boat.

The trip to the club was not a total waste, however. Passing through the clubhouse lobby, I glanced at the bulletin board and happened to spot a flier announcing an October excursion up the river to Cold Spring. It's exactly the trip I've been daydreaming about. And what fun to do it with the fleet! Besides, doing it with people who have made the trip before would offer a nice sense of security. That should reassure Ellen, too—or so I thought.

"Sleep on the boat while it's bouncing up and down all night?" she said when I proposed the idea tonight over supper. "No thanks."

"We'll stay in a hotel. There's a nice place right by the marina."

She softened. "Well . . . that's a possibility."

I was pleased. My hopes rose.

By the next day the weather had turned around completely. The river was no longer a snarling dog with its hackles up, but a sleepy old hound dozing on the carpet. Boats lolled in the hot sun. Flags hung limp from yardarms, halyards rattled idly against masts.

In these conditions there was no point in even uncovering my mainsail. Instead I worked on spiffing up the boat. I sponged out the bilges, swept out the cabin, cleared lines and gear off the sole and coamings, and then scrubbed the decks.

I wanted the boat to look its best for Ellen's visit and our cruise to Cold Spring.

As the date approached, though, I began to wonder if the trip was a good idea. Ellen had yet to set foot on the boat. Was it wise to start her off with a grueling two-day journey? If I was going to win her over to sailing, wouldn't it be smarter to start her off with small steps? An hour or two of sailing on a pleasant afternoon was likely to do more for her confidence than a 48-hour marathon.

In the end the decision was taken out of my hands. While pursuing my wonderful plan for an autumn cruise and a romantic overnight stay in a country inn, I discovered that I was already several months too late. Every hotel for miles around was fully booked for that weekend: prime leaf-peeping time in the Highlands. And since Ellen did not welcome the idea of being rocked to sleep by the rhythms of the river, it seemed I was destined to make the trip on my own— if I made it at all.

October 10th, Thursday:
Who would have thought that raking leaves and clipping shrubs were boating chores? But that's how I spent this afternoon at the club.

It was one of those mellow Indian-summer days, when dry leaves rustle underfoot, the grass has turned dusty brown and every minute of sunlight seems precious because you know there will be fewer of them with each passing day. Too restless to stay at my desk, I was playing hooky from the office so I could spend a few hours outdoors working off my obligations as a member of the club's grounds committee.

With hedge clippers in gloved hands, I was snipping away the wild rose bushes that choked the outer edges of the property. It was easy duty, but I couldn't help feeling that something was out of joint. Who in their right mind joins a boat club to clip brambles and rake leaves? Next year I would try to get a work assignment that took me closer to the water: the mooring committee, maybe, or waterfront.

My reverie was interrupted by the sound of someone's footsteps rustling toward me through the fallen leaves. I looked up to see a ruddy-faced guy with a can of Bud in each hand and a shock of white hair combed across his scalp.

"I thought I'd stop by and see who was pretending to be working so hard," he said, straight-faced. He wore jeans and a work shirt. A pair of work gloves hung out of his back pocket. He offered me a beer.

"Yeah, ain't boating grand?" I said with mock exasperation. I set down the clippers and pulled off my gloves. "Thanks," I said, popping open the can. I took a long swallow.

The man's name was Vincent, aka Vince, Vinny and Vin. I had often seen him around the club but we had never stopped to talk. Today there was time.

Like me, Vin had come late to sailing. A steel worker for over thirty years, he had deferred his boating dreams until his son was out of college. A daughter still had two years to go, but this past spring Vin had decided he'd waited long enough. Scouring the boating magazines and marinas, he had finally found what he wanted: a twenty-year-old O'Day 25. He took the plunge.

"I figured, hey, I'm gonna be sixty, there's not much time left."

"Yeah, mortality sucks," I said. Lifting my can, I clicked it to his. "L'Chaim!"

"Prosit!"

What I found alarming was Vinny's casual admission that he had bought his boat before taking any lessons. Maybe I'm overly cautious, but to my mind this seemed a foolhardy way to start, especially considering all the trouble a guy can get into on the river.

On the other hand, Vinny had spent most of his adult life climbing around on the steel frames of bridges and skyscrapers. He didn't survive for thirty years by being reckless. Learning to sail must have seemed no more difficult to him than guiding a beam into place while perched on a girder hundreds of feet up in the air.

Vinny was about as cool and unflappable as anyone I've met—the kind of guy you can count on in a jam. And like Morris, he was always ready to lend a buddy a hand. Maybe that, too, was a legacy of his job, a case of, "We're in this together, let's help each other out." Or maybe, "I'll help you today because I might need your help tomorrow."

At any rate, after we had finished off our beers, Vinny picked up a rake and, without my even asking, set to work helping clean up the tangle of vines, leaves and branches that littered the ground around me.

I smiled as I thought back again to my first wary assumptions about the kind of people I was likely to meet at a place labeled "boat club." True, not everyone I've encountered there has been a paradigm of good humor and generosity. Stir the surface of any organizational pond and you are sure to turn up a few yucky specimens. But I was lucky in finding guys like Morris and Vinny and Al. I can think of no better companions with whom to share time and the river: to hoist sail on one another's boats, to race for the bridge or to just cruise around on a quiet evening, sipping beer and trading jokes and stories. The love of boats is the one common thread in our lives and it seems to bring out the best in all of us.

October 21, Monday:
This past Saturday was supposed to have been the big day: Ellen's first time on the boat. Having given up the idea of a solitary cruise to Cold Spring—with or without the company of the cruising fleet—I had prepared instead to introduce Ellen to the boat during a brief afternoon outing. And Saturday was to have been the day. But that plan, too, was foiled when the weather turned against us. The forecast

called for wind, rain and cold, and by Friday afternoon the first wave of nasty stuff was already upon us: the temperature dropping, the wind picking up, a fresh dampness thickening the air. It was building up to a classic nor'easter.

"I guess that's it for our cruise," I told Ellen as I gazed gloomily out the window. We had waited too long. The season was coming to a tumultuous end, and I doubted we would get another chance to sail before I had to take the boat away to its winter home.

Ellen made an effort to sound sympathetic, but I had a feeling she was secretly relieved.

By Saturday morning the storm was at full fury. The wind was driving a cold rain horizontally against our windows. Out in the street tree branches skittered along the pavement and blizzards of autumn leaves filled the air.

I donned a heavy sweater, a wool cap and raingear, then drove to the club to see how the boat was doing. Parking in the club lot overlooking the mooring field, I peered out at the river through the rain-streaked windshield. The wind was in a frenzy, blowing the tops off the whitecaps and sending bursts of spray streaming ahead of them. The boats were tossing at their moorings like toys in a bathtub.

Through my binoculars I picked out ADVANCE. She was bucking like a pony with a burr under her saddle, but she seemed to be holding fast to her mooring, taking the waves the way she was meant to. I drove home feeling fairly confident that she would be okay.

As the day wore on, though, the weather got even worse. By afternoon the gutters were running in torrents and the wind was howling like a wounded dog. Despite myself, I could not stop thinking of what it must be doing out on the river.

Let it be, I told myself. Whatever is going to happen will happen. There's nothing you can do about it. But again I drove to the club, drawn by the drama as much as by worry.

Again I parked in the club's upper lot. This time I got out.

Grabbing my binoculars, I made a dash for the shelter of the clubhouse porch. As I ran I heard the shrill whistling of the wind playing a mad fugue in the rigging of the racing boats that were parked on the tarmac down at the water's edge.

The clubhouse porch offered little shelter from the wind and rain, which was blowing in from the east. I took cover inside, knowing there'd be good dry viewing through the picture windows.

A dozen or so other guys had had the same idea. Gathered at the big windows, they held binoculars to their eyes as they peered out at the river. Even the old hands seemed stunned by the fury of the storm.

"Wow, look at that," one man murmured in awe.

"Whew," breathed another.

"Really something," said a third.

Waves were flogging the shoreline. It was high tide, and the river was flinging itself against the bulkheads, sending up great plumes of spray. The piers and the tin boats that were tied to them were being battered mercilessly.

"Hey, Tom, how's your boat doing?" It was Vin. As usual he had a Bud in his hand, and as usual he had an extra one to offer me.

"She's looking good. Thanks." I took the can and popped it open. "How's yours?"

"Aw, the main came loose. I can see it flapping around out there."

"Oh, no. Gee, that's too bad." Raising my binoculars toward where he pointed, I picked out his boat, saw the white sail being whipped to shreds on the boom.

"I don't know how it happened. I tied the sail down with four cords and had the cover on tight. The wind must have got under the front edge somehow. It peeled the cover back like it was a banana."

"Yeah, I see that. That's tough."

Scanning the mooring field, I saw other damage being done as well. A big genoa had worked itself loose and was being ripped from head to clew. On another boat a boom had snapped its tether and was swinging wildly from side to side. Too much of that kind of pressure could bring down the mast.

Down at the water's edge, meanwhile, one of the club's floating docks was being torn loose from the main pier. A tin boat had lost its stern line and was attached to the dock by its bow line alone. Three guys were already at work down there, their yellow slickers bright in the gray light as they bucked the wind and rain in their struggle to get extra lines on the dock and the tin boat.

"I think Morris is down there," Vinny said.

"If anyone would be it'd be Morris."

"You got that right."

As for the rest of us, there was nothing we could do but watch the mayhem and hope for the best.

One piece of advice came through: words of wisdom from an old navy veteran who was at the window with his binoculars: "Every time you leave your boat, you should tie it down as if you're expecting a hurricane. Then you'll be ready for anything."

Ever on the hunt for metaphors, I pondered the man's words, trolling for possible double meanings. Perhaps there was a life lesson here. But I came up empty. Some advice, it seemed, applied only to boats.

The nor'easter made a dramatic ending to a lively season. It was as if the river gods were sending a message: the time had come for us to pack up and get off the river. Winter was on the way.

I set aside the next day, Sunday, for the trip upriver to the marina where I would store ADVANCE. Howard had agreed to help me out, and early on Sunday morning we drove both our cars up to the marina. The storm had blown itself out by then, and although rain still threatened, the wind was down. It looked like we'd have an easy journey.

We left Howard's car parked at the marina for the return trip, then drove to the club in my car. There we headed down to the dock, where we would hitch a ride out to ADVANCE.

The club grounds were a mess. One of the floating docks had been battered to kindling, the gas shed had been blown over, and the launch was under water, sunk at its mooring. A whole platoon of guys was busy cleaning up: tying down the surviving piers, righting the gas shed, clearing away the flotsam that had been tossed up onto the tarmac during the storm's high-water assault. I knew I should stop to help. But today was my only chance to make the trip upriver and I had already arranged for the boat to be hauled out in the middle of the week. I had no choice.

Howard and I got ourselves out to the boat, returned the dinghy to the dock, then set sail northward. I felt like a thief in the night, skulking away from the scene of mayhem. After all the help my buddies had given me, here I was sneaking out on them in their time of need.

But the day was forgiving. A favorable tide and an easterly breeze over the starboard beam were like a parting gift at the end of a wonderful season.

It was mid-afternoon by the time we eased into the marina, sails down, motor pushing us slowly along the channel toward the docks. While Howard got busy hanging fenders over the side, I radioed the office for directions to an empty slip. Steering us through the maze of docks, I crept up on our assigned spot, threw the engine into neutral, and let the boat coast the rest of the way in. My timing was perfect. We glided to a gentle stop, our fenders just kissing the dockside.

"Nicely done, Skipper," Howard said as he stepped off onto the dock and got us tied down.

"Why, thank ye, matey."

We were tucked in between an enormous cabin cruiser on one side and a 30-foot sloop on the other.

"Look at these boats!" Howard exclaimed, a note of awe in his voice. "My god, they're bigger than some houses."

I was busy rigging a spring line to the dock cleat. "Amazing, aren't they?" I said, barely looking up.

Then I caught myself. I remembered how I, too, had been awed the day I came here to take my first class with Diego. I remembered how out of place I had felt, and how the sight of all those enormous and beautiful and unattainable toys had me gawking like a tourist. I remembered admiring their sleek lines, their luxurious details: the shining metalwork and oiled teak; the easy chairs and wet bars glimpsed through Venetian blinds; the bewildering array of color-coded ropes that festooned the topsides of the elegant sloops. I remembered how obscenely covetous I had felt.

Yet even then, possession had not been what I craved so much as the adventurous journeys I would take once I learned the art and skill of sailing. In those early days the thought of owning my own boat—even a small one—had seemed so remote that I barely allowed it to enter my mind.

Now here I was, just a few years later, moving about on my boat—*my boat!*—with hardly a glance to right or left, going about my business as if it were just another hum-drum task in a hum-drum world. I had given hardly a glance at those extraordinary floating homes, those sleek, tall-masted yachts. They no longer held the same sense of mystery or mystique. For now, when I stopped to look around at this sailboat or that one, I knew what I was seeing. And I realized that, given a little practice, I could handle many of these boats. The technology was far more complicated than anything on my little Tanzer, with dozens of lines and whole batteries of winches and cleats and who knows what other gizmos. But when it came to sailing, the principles were basically the same and I knew that I could acquire the skills to manage them if I needed to.

Except that I didn't need to. And *that* was the biggest difference between my first visit to this marina and today's. The truth was, I paid less attention to the boats around me be-cause I was so completely happy with the one I had. Yes, I knew the old saying: that as soon as a man buys a boat he begins to yearn for a bigger one. But that hadn't happened to me. The boat I had right now was all the boat I needed. I envied no man. I wanted nothing more.

# 11

# WINTER WINDS

*"What is more pleasant than a friendly little yacht,*
*a long stretch of smooth water, a gentle breeze, the stars?"*
—William Atkin

I would never say it out loud, but secretly I had to admit it:
I was looking forward to being free of the boat for a few
months. The awful truth was that my sweet sloop could be
a drag at times. Since that joyous day in spring when I had
first cast off from Murdock's mooring and headed out into
the river far too much of my time and energy had gone into
worrying about her. Would she survive the storm that was
headed our way? What if her mooring lines chaffed through
and she drifted away? What if another boat broke loose and
crashed into her? What if the motor quit and left me
stranded? What if a shroud snapped and the mast came
crashing down?

I had done all I could to protect my darling from every
disaster I could think of. So far we had been lucky; no ill
wind had blown our way. But I knew that I wouldn't stop
fretting until she was safely tucked in for the winter.

I felt closer to that longed-for peace of mind when I
heard from the marina that the boat had been hauled out
and was now on land, propped up on jack stands. Good.
Now at least I didn't have to worry about her sinking. What
I did need to do, though, was get her ready for her long winter's nap.

For one thing, I had to empty the toilet's holding tank so
the contents didn't freeze over the winter. The tank, an un-
wieldy balloon of heavy-gauge rubber, was stored in a dark

locker beneath the V-berth. I hadn't paid any attention to it during the summer, but now I needed to take a closer look.

Hauling a ladder over to where the boat stood on its jack stands, I climbed aboard, opened the cabin, then crawled forward with a flashlight, removed the locker cover and peered inside. The tank, which lay like a large black kidney on the bottom of the locker, was connected to the toilet by a couple of thick hoses. To empty it I'd probably have to disconnect the hoses and lift the tank out. But how would I do that without making an unholy mess? I needed advice.

Closing up the locker again before I did something foolish, I busied myself with clearing out the cabin. Cushions, life jackets, radio, window curtains—everything went into the back of the car. Then I drove back home and called Murdock.

"You didn't take her to the pump-out station?" he asked when I told him my dilemma.

"Uh, no. Where's that?"

"There's one right there at the marina. Over at the fuel dock."

"Oh. But the boat's been hauled already. It's up on land."

Ever the gentleman, Murdock restrained himself from laughing at my ignorance and generously offered an alternative. "In that case, just throw some antifreeze into the tank and the toilet. In the spring, when the boat is back in the water, you can run it over to the pump-out."

Brilliant. I had called the right man. On my next visit to the marina I solved the holding tank problem without fuss and, thankfully, without muss.

That reduced my decommissioning jobs to two: hauling the mooring and then getting a cover over the boat before the first snowfall.

Pulling moorings was a fall ritual at every club and marina where winter had teeth. Although the Hudson no longer ices over as often as it used to, no one could predict how bad the next winter would be. A long cold snap could produce a thick sheet of moving ice that could rip away your mooring tackle and leave your mushroom lost on the river bottom, never to be found again. Some at the boat club took their chances and left their mushrooms in, with only a light mooring stick tethered just below the surface to mark the spot for retrieval in the spring. Most of the guys I knew, however, played it safe and pulled their moorings out before the cold weather set in.

But how do you retrieve a three-hundred-pound chunk of iron that is stuck in the mud under twelve feet of water? That was the question I pondered one cool, still Sunday morning in early November, while I raked leaves on the clubhouse lawn.

The day was perfect for pulling the mooring. There was no wind, the water was flat calm. But I wasn't sure this was a job I should tackle on my own. I knew that I'd have to use the cow—the motorized raft I had been introduced to back in the spring, when Kieran helped me put the mooring in. I knew, too, that the cow's overhead winch played a role in the operation. But I had never run either the cow or the winch, and some survival instinct warned me not to attempt it single-handed. Steering the cow was tricky enough; mishandling the winch, with its chains and pulleys and nasty looking hooks could cost me any number of bruises and maybe even a limb or two.

I need not have worried. Since everyone else at the club was now facing the same chore, it was only a matter of time before I found a helping hand.

In this case the hands belonged to a Mutt and Jeff team named Steve and Andy. I found them down at the waterfront, where they were maneuvering the cow up to the bulkhead in preparation for hauling their moorings.

"Sure, hop on," said the tall one when I asked if I could tag along. "We can use another hand. And we can pick your mooring up along the way."

"I don't know how much help I'll be," I said. "I've never done this before."

"That's all right. We'll show you the ropes." He introduced himself as Steve. A beefy, red-faced guy with the nose of a prize fighter and hands to match, he was dressed for serious labor: jeans, flannel work shirt, work boots and heavy leather gloves. "But I'm not the expert. Andy is."

Andy was short, wiry and unsmiling, with a brush cut of white hair and with deep creases in his weathered face. Chin up, one hand grasping the winch frame for support, he immediately assumed command of our clunky little vessel.

"Cast off that line," he ordered as I jumped down to the raft.

"Aye aye, sir," I said and saluted.

I hauled in the line, Steve goosed the throttle and away we went.

Given Andy's craggy looks and his military manner, I figured him for ex-navy, probably officer-grade. He was certainly comfortable giving orders. He was also quick to let us know that he was an elder statesman, and therefore doubly worthy of respect.

"Knees don't work so good when you hit seventy," he muttered as he bent to take a seat on the wooden storage box bolted to the back of the raft.

I gave a sympathetic chuckle, but this seemed to be a mistake.

He glared. "You don't believe me?"

"Hey, whatever you say, Andy."

Apparently it was his age he was strutting, not his infirmities.

"E-Nine," he snapped, pointing his chin toward his mooring.

Steve complied, steering us in the required direction.

As we neared Andy's mooring ball and pickup stick, Steve turned our bow into the current to set up our approach. Easing back on the throttle, he nudged us forward until we ran up to, then over the stick and ball, which rolled under the forward edge of the raft. Seconds later they popped up in the big square hole in the center of the platform, directly beneath the winch.

Andy got down on his knees beside the hole, grabbed the mooring stick and hauled up the ball while Steve held us in position against the current. The old man handed me the mooring line. "Cleat it off."

"Aye aye," I said but skipped the salute this time.

As soon as I got us tethered to the mooring, Steve threw the engine into neutral, then came forward. Together, hand over hand, we hauled up as much as of the mooring line and chain as we could. When it got too heavy Steve jammed the winch hook through one of the lower links and we began winching it up.

"Hey!" Andy barked in my direction.

"What?" His imperious manner was getting annoying.

He pointed at my feet. "Move 'em!"

I looked down. My right foot was planted squarely inside a coil of mooring chain. Quickly I stepped back.

"I saw a guy get both legs torn off by a cable just that way," Andy said. "Aboard ship."

"Navy?" I asked.

"Merchant marine," he growled.

It might have been an optical illusion, but the old curmudgeon seemed to grow three inches when he uttered those words.

The weather held. The water remained calm and the sky clear. The morning's autumn nip gave way to summer warmth as the sun rose toward noon. We were grateful. Our job would have been much harder if the wind had kicked up, tossing us about on our exposed platform.

We took turns hauling on the block and tackle that propelled the winch, pulling the mooring chain up through the hole in the deck one inch at a time. In this way we got most of the chain on deck until there was no more slack below the water line and we could pull no more up. We added as much pressure to the chain as we could. But Andy's mushroom was stuck fast to the bottom. It wouldn't budge.

We tried turning the winch again, increasing the pressure. But instead of the mushroom popping loose, we succeeded only in pulling the raft lower, until water was washing over the deck.

Like terriers watching a rabbit hole we stared down at the place where the chain disappeared into the murky water.

"Wow, that's a real sucker," Steve said.

Andy snorted. "That's the word for it."

"Maybe it's caught on something," I offered.

"Could be," he said. "Lot of crap down there. Old mushrooms. Boats. Trees. Who knows what."

We tried jumping up and down on the deck, hoping to jar the thing loose. Nothing happened. Steve forced another turn on the winch. I stepped further back, afraid the chain might snap and catch me in a bad place. By now the water was washing over our feet.

"Jesus, it ain't . . ."

But then we felt a bump as something gave down below. Suddenly the deck rose to its normal height above the water. The pressure had done its job. The mushroom had popped loose, like a plug pulled from a bathtub drain.

Steve and I took turns at the winch, hauling up more chain and raising the dead weight of the mushroom an inch at a time through twelve feet of water. Finally the eye at the top of the stem broke the surface. A few more pulls and the dish appeared. It was heaped high with thick gray mud. And the mud was loaded with clam shells.

"Hey! Here's our lunch!" said Steve. "Somebody get the pot boiling."

"Nah, it's just shells," Andy said, ever the realist.

Getting down on his rum knees again, he leaned over the dish and started shoveling the mud back into the river. While he worked, Steve got the motor in gear and headed us off toward his mooring, where we repeated the process.

Steve's mushroom came up out of the mud without any trouble. As I worked the winch, he guided the chain over the winch pulley with a gloved hand. Slowly, one link at a time, the heavy mooring chain rose out of the water. The three of us watched as if hypnotized, waiting for the top of the mushroom stem to break the surface. Only when Steve let out a yelp did we realize just how distracted we had become. Looking up, I saw that Steve's fingers were caught between the chain and the pulley. Quickly I reversed the winch, freeing his hand.

"Jesus, are you all right?" I asked.

"I think so." Because he wasn't groaning I thought he might be in shock. But he was lucky. Only the tip of his glove had been mashed, not flesh and bone.

My mushroom came up without a hitch and as soon as it was safe on deck Steve headed us back toward shore. Our clothes were wet and spattered with mud. The new cotton gloves I had brought for raking leaves were soaked and shredded from hauling rusty chains. My white running shoes were river-bottom gray. But since no mushrooms got dropped on any toes and no one fell overboard, we rated the operation a success. Even Old Stone Face cracked a smile. As for me, I was just thankful that I had not attempted to do the job on my own. There could have been blood as well as mud on the deck. I had to admit that while self-reliance may be a virtue, it does have its limits.

Back at the bulkhead, we used a dockside hoist to winch the mushrooms off the cow and up onto the tarmac. Following Steve and Andy's example, I fired up the power washer and blasted the barnacles and mud off my chain, pennants and mushroom, then used a rolling winch to wheel the whole rig over to the "mushroom farm," an out-of-the-way corner of the property, where it would sit out the winter in company with a few dozen others just like it.

Job done, I dragged my muddy carcass home for a hot shower, clean clothes, a good stiff drink and that happy realization that I now had only one boat job left to do. After that I'd be a free man again.

Snow and ice can wreck havoc with boats. Hairline cracks in the fiberglass can be pried open. Caulking hardens and splits. Melt water seeps beneath fittings and around window edges, where it rots the balsa core of the fiberglass laminate.

Knowing this, I grew anxious to get the boat covered before winter kicked in. Already the nighttime temperatures were slipping below freezing. We'd have snow before long. I had to hurry.

Getting a cover over the boat should have been easy: throw on a tarp and tie it down. But as I had been learning all summer long, nothing on a boat is ever easy or quick the first time around.

The trick was to stretch the tarp in such a way that water, ice and snow would slide off rather than pooling in low spots. A gallon of water weighs eight pounds. Twenty or thirty gallons concentrated in one small area could add enough hanging weight to split the tarp and dump all that water into the boat, where it could do its insidious work.

Looking around the yard at the marina, I saw that some owners had solved the problem by building elaborate A-frame tents over their boats, complete with sloping sidewalls. But at the time I had neither the hours nor the patience to undertake a major carpentry job. Instead, I would use the materials at hand.

The ridgepole of my tent would be the mast, which had been taken down and now lay lengthwise across the top of the boat, its ends lashed to the safety rails at the bow and stern. No big construction job would be required. All I'd need to do was drape the tarp over the mast and tie it down.

I climbed the ladder to the deck. Right away I knew I'd

have a fight on my hands. The wind was up and singing in the rigging of every boat in the yard.

I clambered into the cockpit, braced myself against the cabin bulkhead and tried to shake the folds out of the big blue plastic tarp. But unfurling it in this wind was like trying to wrestle an armload of crazed chickens into submission. At times I was afraid I'd be blown right off the top of the boat. But I managed to secure first one corner, then another.

It took a couple trips up and down the ladder, but eventually I had all four corners tied under the boat. The object then was to tie down all the loose ends, so that the wind had nothing to grab onto. At the same time I knew I'd need to leave openings at the bow and stern so that the air could circulate under the tarp and through the cabin, helping to forestall condensation and the mold that went with it.

When I finally had everything tied down, I stood back to examine my handiwork. I could see no loose ends. But I was troubled by the way the forward part of my tent pancaked over the mast and spreaders rather than rising to a nice peak. All those flat surfaces would surely collect rain and snow. But there was nothing more I could do about it just then. The light was fading, the sky was turning a cold gray blue, and I was out of time. I'd have to return the next weekend to make adjustments. Until then I'd just have to hope for the best.

It took me not one, two or even three but four more trips to the boatyard, a half hour each way, before I was satisfied that the tarp was set right. Anyone would have thought I had nothing else to do in my spare time. By the end I was thoroughly fed up with my own obsession. But I was too full of fears about what might happen to my sweet ADVANCE if I didn't do the job properly. So I kept at it, trying the cover this way and that, undoing it, redoing it.

One time I noticed that the tarp's metal grommets were chaffing the hull. I taped and padded them. Another time I discovered that snow had found a new low place in which to settle, and the weight was pulling the tarp down between the wooden supports I'd built. When I climbed the ladder to see what was happening inside the tent, I found what looked like a nursery of bloated blue udders hanging from the tent roof. I only hoped none of them would burst and spill their contents before I had a chance to come back with some lumber and build a proper tent, peaked roof and all. Clearly my shortcut approach was not working.

On my next trip I pulled off the tarp and went to work building a frame of 2x2s, as I should have done right from the beginning. The frame rose to a high point at the crosstrees on the mast.

I secured the frame to the stanchions and safety rails using the handyman's friend: duct tape. I stood a short piece of 2x4 on the cabin top, making it the highest point on the boat. Across this I laid a ridgepole that extended from one end of the boat to the other. Over this structure I draped the tarp, creating a tent that looked something like a squashed teepee, with a high point at the center and with the sides falling away on all sides. It wasn't an elegant setup, but it looked like it would solve my drainage problem.

Mostly it did. There was only one hitch, which I discovered on my next visit. Climbing the ladder and looking in through the ventilation opening I had left at the stern, I saw that the weather had found another sneaky way to outfox me. A recent rainstorm had not only dropped water from above but had blown it in through my clever air vent. Inch-thick patches of ice now lay in the cockpit: both on the seat and in the footwell. I could almost hear the ice digging its greedy fingers into the boat's laminate.

Needing to readjust the tarp yet again, I untied enough of the cover to allow myself to scramble aboard. Under the tarp the world glowed arctic blue, the way glaciers must look from the inside. On hands and knees I crawled forward to check the cabin. Everything was dry except for a little ice in the bilge beneath the floorboards, where condensation runoff had collected. But there was nothing major to worry about.

Next I checked the locker under the forward V-berth, where the holding tank for the toilet was stored. On my previous visit I had noticed a glint of water down there in the darkness, beneath the tank. Now, peering in again, I thought the water was higher than before. Damn. Where was it coming from? Condensation? Leaks at the joints where the deck met the hull?

I'd have to come back in a week or two to check the hold again. If more water had come in by then, I knew I'd have to do some repairs in the spring, caulking the joints. But no sewage odors were coming from the toilet tank and that was encouraging. Something, at least, was under control.

Retreating to the cockpit, I took one more look around. That's when I noticed that the plastic tarp had worn through at the point where it rubbed against the tops of the lifeline stanchions—a perfect opening for wind and water. Obviously I needed to pad the tops of the stanchions. And I had just the material to do it with: carpet remnants. How did I happen to have carpet remnants on hand? Having saved a large strip from a carpet job at home, I had followed a tip from a friend and used cut-off squares to prevent chaffing of the tarp ties against the boat's hull. Those remnants would work equally well to pad the stanchions. Folding aside the tarp, I pulled out my trusty duct tape and secured the carpet bits in place. Then I pulled the cover back over the boat and tied it down, confident at last that I had done everything I could to protect ADVANCE from the ravages of winter.

Wrong again. During the months that followed I returned to the boatyard repeatedly to check on ADVANCE and to tinker with the cover. In the wake of every high wind or snowstorm, I would be up at the yard, checking things out. Was the cover still secure or had it been ripped to shreds?

Was the boat still upright on its jack stands or had the ground settled, shifting its footings?

Looking back with all the benefits of hindsight, I can pinpoint that winter as the time I finally recognized a sad truth about myself: I had turned into a first-class worrywart. At the office, while meeting with my colleagues, I'd find myself nodding and seeming to listen as they discussed the fine points of some important project or other. But my head was at the boat yard, pondering my latest maintenance dilemma: Maybe if I built in some more supports under the tarp . . .

"Don't you think so, Tom?" someone was asking.

"Oh, absolutely," I agreed, hoping I sounded like I knew what they'd been talking about.

I shivered. Keep on like this and I risked acquiring major demerits on my next performance appraisal.

It was pathetic. Apparently by acquiring a boat I had doomed myself to a permanent state of anxiety. Day and night fretful thoughts yipped like schnauzers at the corners of my mind, disturbing my thoughts, unsettling my dreams. Yet short of dumping the boat, there was no way out. I was committed. The responsibility was mine and would not go away till Death did us part.

The odd thing was, none of this made me unhappy. I knew that the care and worry would be for the best if it meant that ADVANCE got through to spring safely. Besides, I enjoyed the time I spent visiting the boatyard.

There I'd be, scrambling over the deck as I readjusted the frame once more or retied the cover. The sun would be warm on my back and the river breeze cool on my cheeks. Now and then I'd be interrupted by the honking of geese as they passed in formation high overhead, or by the blast of a horn from the gypsum plant next door, where a freighter was edging its way out into the channel after unloading its cargo. Looking up from my task, I'd suddenly remember where I was and thank my lucky stars as I paused to savor the world around me: the diamond-hard sunlight dancing on the river;

the leafy earth smells rising from the nearby marsh; the sight of a hound, chin on its paws, drowsing in the shadow of its master's boat.

Even on land, perched high and dry on her jack stands, ADVANCE brought magic to my life.

There must have been a few days that winter when I did not give a thought to the boat or to sailing. Around the holidays I must have had gifts on my mind, and parties and family celebrations. Probably I thought about work a little, too; some pesky year-end deadline was surely breathing down my neck. I couldn't swear to it, though. Looking back, it seems that I had hardly finished getting the boat snugged down under her cover than I began thinking about what I needed to do to get ADVANCE ready for launching in the spring.

For one thing, the keel needed serious attention. River brine had taken its toll, leaching away big patches of blue bottom paint and exposing whole archipelagos of rust and decay. Some gouges were quite deep and would require major skin grafts.

ADVANCE's topsides, too, looked worse for wear. Back in the spring, when I bought her, she had been spotless. Murdock had obviously worked hard to make her that way. Now it was up to me. The hull and decks, streaked and grimy thanks to exposure to the weather and to air-borne pollution, would need a good cleaning and waxing. The teak drop boards and handrails, once a lovely golden brown, were now dingy gray; they needed to be cleaned and refinished.

But where would I find the time to do it all? Who would teach me to do it? Washing and waxing the hull didn't scare me. I had done cars often enough; how much different could this be? But the other jobs were daunting. I had no idea how to fill and fare those gouges in the keel, no idea what materials to use. And what about the teak? Would I have to sand it down first or just clean it? Was it better to treat it with oil or with varnish? Again I needed help.

Help came in the mail, in the form of a flier from the marina where the boat was stored. The flier listed spring recommissioning services, including cleaning and waxing, bottom painting and teak refinishing. I gasped at the prices and made up my mind then and there to tackle the cleaning and waxing on my own. But I also decided to leave the keel work to the experts. The price was steep but not as steep as the learning curve I'd face if I tried to do the job myself. I called the marina office, asked them to fax me a work order, filled it out and sent it back with my deposit. Easy. All it took was money. But these days, with my latest royalty check tucked away in the bank, I could spare the money easier than I could spare the time.

"I have this friend who has a boat, and he used to say . . ."

My stomach sank, taking with it a good chunk of tuna-on-rye.

I was having lunch in the office cafeteria with one of the guys from the marketing department and I had begun telling him about the boat: the pleasures of it but also the work I faced and what it cost to maintain it. At the mention of cost his eyes brightened. I just knew what was coming next: the most popular cliché in the boating lexicon. And I wasn't wrong.

"He used to say that a boat is a hole in the water into which you pour money."

The first time I heard that line I had laughed. What did I know? New to sailing, I had been blissfully unaware of just how often every sailor is doomed to hear it.

By now, all I could manage in response was a tolerant smile. "Yes, I've heard that," I said, and quickly changed the subject.

If only someone had warned me. I had spent hundreds of dollars on sailing instruction. I had sat through many hours of classes, learning tactics and strategy, boating safety and coastal navigation. At every step I had heard cautionary tales about the many perils that sailors are likely to encounter, from collisions in the fog and sudden storms to equipment failures and plotting errors.

From no book or teacher, however, did I hear a word of caution about the most common hazard of nautical life: The storm of bromides that awaits every sailor who ventures into a conversation about boats with non-sailors.

I began hearing the "hole in the water" line as soon as I started talking to friends and colleagues about my yearning to own a boat. I also began hearing the one about "The happiest day of a man's life," etc., etc. One friend, at least, was slightly more original. "I know a guy," he said, "who says owning a boat is like standing in a cold shower tearing up hundred dollar bills."

Usually such jibes were uttered with a hail-fellow camaraderie. Sometimes they were spoken with a self-satisfied smirk that said, "*You* may want to throw your money away on a boat, but *I* would never do anything so stupid."

At other times, though, my friends genuinely seemed to think they were doing me a favor, warning me against jumping into something I would later regret. And in the early days I appreciated their concern, I really did. But once I made the leap and actually became a boat owner, the breeze of well-meaning platitudes grew to a gale, blowing away any forbearance I still possessed.

It amazes me how people who know nothing else about boats seem to have the line about a "hole in the water" just waiting on the tips of their tongues. I'll bet Ulysses heard it from his shore-bound pals. And I can just imagine poor Christopher Columbus approaching King Ferdinand and Queen Isabella for money to buy a few boats. "You know," says the king, "I have this friend, a duke, who has a boat and he says a boat is a hole in the water into which . . ." And so forth.

No wonder sailors tend to avoid talking about boats with anyone but other sailors. It's better than having to chuckle politely every time the old chestnut drops into your lap.

Well, there will be no more chuckles from me. I am putting my foot down. I may not be able to cork the cliché, but I have hit on a plan to profit from it. The next time some wise guy grins and says, "I've got this friend who . . ." I will stop him in his tracks. "Wait," I will demand. "If you're about to say what I think you are, it's going to cost you."

I figure if I can collect a dollar every time I hear that infamous line, I'll soon have enough in the bank to buy a new winch. Or maybe I'll get the knot meter fixed. Or, no, wait, what about an autopilot? Or better yet . . .

On the slush-covered heels of a cold and wet March, April came in warm and sunny. Wanting to believe that the snow was gone for good, I loaded a ladder and a tool box into the car and drove up to the marina yard, eager to get ADVANCE ready for launching.

The place was literally buzzing. Sanding machines and electric drills rasped and chattered as boat owners and their friends attacked keels, hulls and topsides. Pungent chemicals wafted on the air. Buddies called to buddies. Dogs chased one another around the yard. Occasionally in the lull of racket I could hear the trill of a redwing in the nearby marsh.

Having tucked the car in between ADVANCE and the boat next door, I unloaded the ladder, set it against the transom, and climbed to the cockpit. I peeled back the cover, opening the decks once more to the sun and air. Caught by the wind, the tarp flapped and flew like a great blue bird wing.

I quickly dismantled the frame, then spent two hours stringing a new antenna cable through a hole at the mast base, then back through the cabin to the VHF. It was a good piece of work, with the cable nicely hidden away under the seats and secured to the bulkheads. If you weren't looking for it you wouldn't even know it was there.

Over the next couple of weekends I tackled the teak handrails with cleaning fluid, a wire brush and sandpaper, then painted them with teak oil and buffed them to a mellow glow. I washed the hull with soap and water, scrubbed it with cleaning compound, then waxed it until it shone mirror-bright in the spring sunshine. During the weekdays while I sat at my desk at the office and attended meetings and wrote memos, the marina crew was busy doing what my salary was paying them to do: scraping, faring and painting the keel and the hull below the waterline.

Finally, one Monday afternoon, the phone on my desk brought me the news I had been waiting for: ADVANCE had been launched. She was now tied up at a slip. I could come and get her whenever I was ready.

I was on my feet, ready to cheer. "That's great," I said into the receiver. "Thanks for letting me know."

All I needed now was a few more days of good weather. If I could get my mooring set in the next day or two, I could bring the boat down to Nyack the following weekend.

Giddy with excitement, I hurried down the hall to my friend Jim's office, to share the good news. "The boat's in the water," I told him.

Jim, who might get excited about a hole-in-one but not about much else, greeted my enthusiasm with sardonic restraint. "Hmm," he said, pondering as he leaned back in his chair and stared up at the ceiling: "'His boat's in the water but . . .' It's almost an aphorism, but it needs something. 'His boat's in the water but . . .'"

I laughed and we spent the next few minutes groping for the right line. But an ending eluded us.

Later in the day, though, on a hunch, I called the yard manager back, just to make sure that the boat was indeed ready to go and that all systems had been checked out: radio, mast light, running lights.

"Oh yes, it's in the water," she confirmed. "But they haven't stepped the mast yet."

"Oh," I said, suddenly deflated. "When will they get to it?"

"Not until next week at the earliest."

My disappointment was the mirror image of my earlier enthusiasm. I wouldn't be sailing as soon as I had hoped. When I thought more about it, though, I realized that the delay had some benefit: It would give me more time to get the mooring in and well set on the river bottom.

There was another plus as well: I now had the ending for Jim's aphorism: "His boat's in the water but his mast ain't up."

Driving home over the bridge that evening, I glanced upriver toward the boat club and smiled at the sight I saw there. Just offshore, where a few weeks earlier I had seen nothing but empty water, now floated a dainty armada of white hulls and swaying masts. It was as if a flock of birds had returned from wintering in the south and taken up their roosts on the river once more.

With an effort I tore my eyes away. (*Careful! Watch the road!*) But that splendid vision remained imprinted on my brain, along with the happy knowledge that my own sweet bird would soon be joining the flock.

That evening I called Vinny and arranged to meet him at the dock the next day after work, so we could give each other a hand getting our moorings set.

The day dawned clear and cool, an encouraging sign. But at the office I had a hard time concentrating. Worries kept flitting across my mind like moths in an attic. Would the weather hold? Would the wind be too strong to maneuver the cow out to the drop site? Would I have time to get the job done before sunset? Would Vinny be there as promised?

He was there all right. So was a guy named Karl, who was also looking for help with his mooring. This was great. Two sets of hands were good for this job, but three sets were better: one to steer the cow, one to manage the mooring, the third to keep a lookout for safety's sake.

A threesome also multiplied our chances of having a good time. As we wrestled our moorings over to the bulkhead, then hooked each one in turn to the hoist and lowered it onto the cow, our high spirits kept popping to the surface. We joked and bantered, relishing this first chance of the season to be out on the water.

We were three middle-aged men: a construction engineer, an accountant, an editor. We were solid citizens all: responsible family men; professionals with long experience in our fields; respected members of our communities. We supported youth groups and sat on the boards of charitable organizations. People counted on us and we took our obligations seriously. Out there on the water, though, as we maneuvered the rickety old motorized raft through the mooring field, we were giddy Huck Finns, free once more of the land that had bound us through the long winter months.

The evening sun warmed our cheeks and a damp breeze out of the south carried the sweet tang of the sea to our noses. As we putt-putted toward the numbered orange Tide bottle that marked Vinny's mooring position, he checked the chains and lines at his feet, arranging the tackle so that it would play out neatly over the side, with no chance of getting snagged or tangled.

"How's it look?" Karl called from back at the motor controls.

"Hold her there," Vinny shouted.

"We're right on the mark," I added.

Stretched full length on the steel deck, I reached over the side, grabbed the Tide bottle, and got ready to haul it aboard. Vinny rolled his big iron mushroom to the edge of the raft and shoved it over. It hit the water with a satisfying splash, dragging the mooring chain down after it.

He straightened and spread his arms wide and proclaimed to all the world: "Summer is here!"

*"It takes several years for anyone to learn to handle a yacht reasonably well, and a lifetime to admit how much more there is to learn."*
—Maurice Griffiths

Since the start of that new season, my boat and I have welcomed many other new seasons. We have voyaged farther than I would have dared during that first year. Each new adventure has emboldened me, expanding my imagination, enticing me further: down river, beneath the bridges and beyond the river's mouth to the outer harbor to where the ocean begins.

I am a far better sailor now than when I started. Experience and persistence have paid off. I know more about my boat, more about wind and water, more about myself. These days I go out in winds that once would have kept me rooted ashore in fear. I am more confident, and that has made me a better skipper. These days my guests are less likely to hear me mutter things like "Oh, no," and "Holy shit!" Partly that's because I know what I'm doing. Partly it's because when glitches crop up—and they always do—I try to keep my expletives to myself.

Has the wind come up, threatening to push the boat over on its side? No need for my guests to be nervous. I simply ask one of them to loosen "that line over there" while directing another to haul on "that other line, the smaller one by your left hand." Then, with sails safely reefed, we steady up nicely and sail for home on an even keel.

Has the motor crapped out again? No problem. We'll come into the mooring under sail, and do a neat job of it, too.

My guests seem impressed with my skill and are happier sailors than when I first took them out.

But there is another difference as well: These days the boat I sail is not the same one I started with.

One November morning a couple of years ago, a vicious nor'easter blew through our valley. It arrived a month after we'd been battered by the backwash of Hurricane Floyd. ADVANCE came through that storm with only minor injuries. What had caused them was uncertain, but the bent bow pulpit, the scrapes on her port rail and a nearly severed shroud suggested that a nearby boat had been torn from its mooring. It then got hung up on ADVANCE before breaking free and continuing on to whatever fate awaited it downriver. Six or eight boats were lost from the club that day.

The insurance company reimbursed me in full for the repairs to ADVANCE, and I had just finished getting everything fixed up when the nor'easter hit us with a sucker punch.

I knew it was coming. The weather reports were all too clear: *". . . sustained winds of fifty-miles-an-hour . . . gusts up to seventy."*

Afraid of another collision, I got on the phone and reserved dock space at the town marina, where the boat might at least be sheltered from the worst of the wind, not to mention from wayward boats. But I was too late. I left my office early that afternoon, but by the time I got down to the waterfront, the wind was blowing so hard and the seas running so high that I doubted I could safely maneuver a dinghy over to ADVANCE. From where I stood on shore I could see her being tossed around by the turbulent seas. Even if I managed to get out to her, I'd still have to secure the bouncing dinghy to the pitching boat, then somehow get myself aboard. Then I'd have to maneuver the boat and dinghy over to the shelter of the marina. It was impossible. I had no choice. All I could do was cross my fingers and trust to fate.

That night, as predicted, the wind blew hard and long: fifty miles an hour, sustained over four hours or more. It was brutal. By morning the streets of our village were littered with downed branches. Some areas of town were without power. I wanted to check the boat, to see how it had survived the blow. But I didn't have time. I had to hit the road for an early-morning meeting at the office.

I returned from that meeting to find a message on my office phone: "This is John from Towboat U.S. Give me a call as soon as you can."

My stomach lurched. Uh, oh, I thought, this can't be good news.

It wasn't. ADVANCE had somehow broken free of her mooring and was on the rocks at Croton Point, five miles upriver. The Towboat guy had spotted her while pursuing another runaway. Thanks to the Boat/U.S. insurance sticker on ADVANCE's mast and the registration number on her bows the Towboat guy had been able to track me down.

My poor boat. As I listened to John's description, my heart sank. How she had broken loose he couldn't tell. Her pennants were still attached to the bow cleats and were stretched taut from where they connected to the mooring chain. Part of the chain, too, was stretched tight across the rocks and down into the murky water. But whether the mushroom was also down there, John wasn't sure. Either the chain itself was caught on the rocks or it was being held tight by the weight of the mushroom.

"You mean it might have dragged a three-hundred-pound mushroom all the way up the river?" I asked.

"It happens."

"How bad is the damage to the boat?"

"I can't tell yet. I'm sending a diver down to see if the hull has been punctured. I'll give you a call back as soon as I know anything."

Distracted, full of anxiety, I waited for his next report. Finally, unable to bear the suspense, I called back. His news was good. He had the boat in tow and was heading for his home port in Tarrytown, three miles across the river from

Nyack. That was where I found her when I hurried over after work.

I felt like weeping at the sight that greeted me. After all the love and attention I had lavished on her, after all the adventures we had shared, my little boat looked as if she'd been beaten up by some hateful bully. Deep gouges scarred her hull and topsides. One of her windows and part of her cabin top had been punched in. Her rudder was mangled and her bow coaming was shredded. The thought crossed my mind that maybe it really had been bad luck to change her name.

Still, on the whole I was lucky. If the Towboat guy hadn't happened to turn up when he did and pull her off the rocks, ADVANCE would have been battered to pieces during the next high tide. As it was, there seemed to be a good chance she could be repaired and sailed again. Certainly she was in better shape than many other boats that had been wrecked during the two storms: boats whose carcasses now littered the shores of the Hudson, where they were rapidly being stripped by scavengers looking for parts and equipment.

But getting ADVANCE back into useable condition would take either a lot of work or a lot of money and I had not the heart for either. I felt defeated. Maybe this was a message. Maybe it was time for me to quit sailing. Between continued problems with the motor, and a seemingly endless litany of demands ADVANCE made on my time and pocketbook, maybe the best thing I could do was to scrap her—call a salvager to haul her away and break her up for parts. On the other hand . . .

As the shock of the loss began to wear off, I realized that this latest misfortune might actually be an opportunity in disguise.

A few months earlier I had taken a weekend cruise on Vinny's new twenty-eight-footer. Ever since then, I had been toying with the idea of trading up to something similar. A bigger boat made sense for the longer cruises I hoped to take.

I had seen first-hand the differences in comfort and elbow-room between my twenty-two footer and a boat just a few feet longer. Why not take the leap?

Scoping out the possibilities, I quickly discovered that with just a little more money than the insurance company was giving me for ADVANCE—they called her a total loss and sent me a check for almost the full amount that I had paid for her—I could move up to something slightly newer and slightly bigger.

I now sail a Catalina 25 that is almost as many years old as she is long in feet. I named her KÄRA FLICKA, Swedish for "Dear Girl," in honor of my Stockholm-born daughter-in-law—the only other person in the family who enjoys sailing as much as I do.

The new boat has already taken me on longer voyages than I had ever dared in ADVANCE. I like her stability and her roominess, and so does Ellen, who has been out on her more often in one season than she ever was in all the years I owned ADVANCE.

And what of ADVANCE? What would be the fate of my sweet first boat, my partner in daydreams? Would she have to be put down like an injured horse? Would the salvagers take her away and chop her into little pieces? At first I could see no alternative. Who would want to buy a boat that was in such bad shape?

But a funny thing happened. That winter, a man who had never before owned a boat went nosing around the marina where ADVANCE was stored. Curious, he asked Nick, the yard manager, if he knew of any used boats for sale—something cheap. No, it didn't matter if it needed work. He was handy and could do most of the jobs himself.

Nick called to tell me the news. "He'll probably take it off your hands for a couple of hundred dollars," Nick said. "His name is Walter. He's a new member of the boat club."

I called Walter and we quickly came to terms. He gave me a check, I signed the registration over to him and that was that. ADVANCE had a new owner—and a happier fate than I would have expected on that grim day when I first saw her beaten and bruised after her time on the rocks.

As promised, Walter fixed her up. You can still see where she was damaged—especially in the discolored fiberglass repairs to the cabin top and window. But I have no complaints. I am just grateful that she is afloat and not lying in pieces in some salvage yard.

I would pass her sometimes at the boat club, on my way to or from my own mooring. Although I was completely delighted with KÄRA FLICKA, I couldn't help but feel a surge of pride and affection at the sight of ADVANCE, with her graceful lines, her bow lifting on the swells as if she just can't wait to be let loose to run and play. It pleased me to see her alive and well. She was, after all, my first sweetheart, and as with all first loves, she's the one I will remember best.

BOOKS:

Adams, Arthur G., *The Hudson River Guidebook*. New York: Fordham University Press, 1996

Bedell, Cornelia, *Now and Then and Long Ago in Rockland County, New York*. New City, New York: The Historical Society of Rockland County, 1992

Boyle, Robert H., *The Hudson River: A natural and unnatural history*. New York: WW Norton & Company, Inc., 1979

Carmer, Carl, *The Hudson*. New York: Fordham University Press, 1939, 1995

Cronin, John and Kennedy, Robert F., *The Riverkeepers*. New York: Scribners, 1997

Coote, John O., ed., *The Norton Book of the Sea*. New York: WW Norton & Company, Inc., 1989

Duncan, Roger F., et. al., *The Cruising Guide to the New England Coast*. New York: Norton, 1997

Dunwell, Frances F., *The Hudson River Highlands*. New York: Columbia University Press, 1991

Fontenoy, Paul E., *The Sloops of the Hudson River: A Historical and Design Survey*. Mystic, CT: Mystic Seaport Museum, in Association with the Hudson River Maritime Museum, 1994

Lane, Carl, *How to Sail.* New York: WW Norton & Company, Inc., 1947

Maloney, Elbert S., *Chapman Piloting: Seamanship & Small Boat Handling.* New York: Hearst Marine Books, 1999

Reed, John, *The Hudson River Valley.* New York: Crown, 1960

*South Nyack Centennial, 1878-1978.* South Nyack Historical Society

Vaitses, Alan, *What Shape is She In?: A Guide to the Surveying of Boats.* New York: McGraw-Hill, 1990

Van Zandt, Roland, *Chronicles of the Hudson.* Black Dove Press.


WEBSITES:

The New Netherland Museum: www.newnetherland.org/history.htm

Hudson River Museum: www.ulster.net/~hrmm

*Other books of interest:*

## SAILING LANGUAGE
by Elliott Dunlap Smith & Thomas R. Moore
Like all human endeavors, sailing has its own unique language, a rich
terminology reflecting the ancient origin and sophisticated nature of the
sport. *Sailing Language* is your key to its proper usage. More than just
another dictionary, it's an entertaining, literate compendium of the language
of boats and sailing. It contains the vocabulary sailors use, carefully arranged
for quick and easy reference.

## MAINSAIL TO THE WIND
### A Book of Sailing Quotations
by William Galvani
"...once you start reading this book, you're hooked." *48° North*
"...a book for all those who love the thrill of sailing the oceans, or just dream
of it." *Sailing & Yachting (SA)*
"...both a valuable resource and fun to browse." *Sailing*
"The author has gathered the best and most memorable...in this book."
*Latitudes & Attitudes*

## CATBOAT SUMMERS
by John E. Conway
Chronicles a decade's worth of adventure in New England waters through a
series of short tales, each recounting one of the Conways' many extraordinary
experiences aboard their 100-year-old wooden catboat, BUCKRAMMER. From
the hilariously ill-fated participation of a fleet of catboats in Boston Harbor's
Sail 2000 Parade to a chilling, phantasmal encounter amidst fog and darkness
and even a pilgrimage to the yard where BUCKRAMMER was born, readers
will be enthralled by Conway's compelling narrative and whimsical humor.

## IF *THE SHOE* FITS
### The Adventures of a Reluctant Boatfrau
by Rae Ellen Lee
"...guided by love and sustained by humor...warm, human and very funny..."
Linda Ridihalgh, editor, *Living Aboard*
"Lee shares her cruising adventures with deep personal
reflection and humor." *Offshore*

## CARIBBEAN CRUISING
### Your Guide to the Perfect Sailing Holiday
by Jane Gibb with John Kretschmer
Expert advice on ideal cruising locations, choosing the best boat, weather
forecasts, equipment, clothes, supplies, expenses, communications, power
needs, health, legal formalities, and much more.
"...delights as it informs...you'll find all the information you are likely to
need..." *Sailing & Yachting (SA)*

**SHERIDAN HOUSE**
*America's Favorite Sailing Books*
www.sheridanhouse.com